"Gibler provides us with a rare integratio[...]
Grounded in a theology of creation, the t[...]
well as the science behind the new universe story, she approaches her study of
the Sacrament of Baptism through biblical, patristic, and cosmic insights into
water, oil, and fire. The sacrament comes alive in both its human and cosmic
dimensions. Her work reflects ways in which science, theology, and spirituality can all complement each other. It is truly a cosmocentric sacramental
spirituality."

—Donald Goergen, OP
St. Dominic Priory
St. Louis, Missouri

"Father Thomas Berry, CP, the foremost eco-theologian of our time, concluded after a lifetime of study that Pierre Teilhard de Chardin, SJ, was the
most important Christian thinker since St. Paul. More than half a century
after Teilhard's death a number of Catholic scholars are deeply engaged in this
transition from modern Christianity's focus on human-human relationships to
a cosmological Catholicism keenly aware of nature as the primary revelation
of God. With the strength of her intellectual synthesis and the depth of her
scholarship, Dr. Linda Gibler, OP, is at the cutting edge of this transformation.
Drawing from both the most ancient wisdom of the Catholic tradition and the
new understanding of the universe from contemporary science, *From the
Beginning to Baptism* enables its readers to understand the ways in which
Baptism is a powerful entrance into that primordial Energy that once gave
birth to the galaxies and later ignited the life in the first cells."

—Brian Swimme, PhD
California Institute of Integral Studies

"Linda Gibler's readable work is both original and consequential. I know of no
other work that attempts to provide such a carefully developed bridge between
contemporary cosmological and scientific understandings of nature on the
one hand, and sacramentality as liturgically understood on the other. Highly
recommended."

—John F. Haught, PhD
Senior Fellow, Science & Religion
Woodstock Theological Center
Georgetown University, Washington, DC

From the Beginning to Baptism

Scientific and Sacred Stories of Water, Oil, and Fire

Linda Gibler

Foreword by David N. Power

M̲
G

A Michael Glazier Book

LITURGICAL PRESS
Collegeville, Minnesota

www.litpress.org

A Michael Glazier Book published by Liturgical Press

Cover design by David Manahan, OSB. Photo of the Red Sea area, photos.com.

1   2   3   4   5   6   7   8

Library of Congress Cataloging-in-Publication Data

Gibler, Linda.
    From the beginning to Baptism : scientific and sacred stories of water, oil, and fire / Linda Gibler ; foreword by David N. Power.
        p.   cm.
    "A Michael Glazier book."
    Includes bibliographical references and index.
    ISBN 978-0-8146-5673-0
    1. Baptism—Catholic Church—History.   2. Sacramentals.   I. Title.

BX2205.G53   2010
234'.161088282—dc22

2009043036

To my mentors

CONTENTS

Chapter Three: Fire   75

Chapter Four: Cosmocentric Sacramentality   111

Bibliography   131

Subject Index   135

Scriptural Index   137

FOREWORD

David N. Power, OMI

Dr. Linda Gibler provides us in this book with a rich study of the use of water, oil, and fire in the Christian liturgy, attending to their use in a variety of traditions and over extended periods of time and in a very special way to the opening of current new perspectives on their place in the human story. Alongside bread and wine, these are the earthly elements most central to liturgical action, and reflection on her work may help with a liturgical renewal through the proper and holy use of the things which provided by Earth sustain human life.

Religious traditions, inclusive in a particular way of the Judeo-Christian, have always worshiped God and divine presence through things of Earth. They weave into celebration the most common elements needed for existence, such as bread, wine, oil, water, fire. These in the first place reflect human life, for they are things by which we live, which we share among ourselves, and in which we share Earth's own life. They are necessary to existence, to life, and to life in human communities. Their production involves human beings with the ground which they inhabit and with the rhythms of the Universe, reflective thus not only of human life lived in common but also of the riches of Earth and of cosmic wonders. In these days we have three reasons to be newly conscious of this.

First is the awareness of how liturgical celebrations have been impoverished because of ignorance of longer traditions and their abundant, generous, and symbolic use of all the elements listed above. Gibler points in tradition to the loss of an appreciation of poetic prayer and to the growth of attention to secondary actions that draw attention away from these things and their symbolic use. This meant an impoverishment of the sacramental element and the sacramental action. From liturgical history we know that this went with the efforts, in some periods perhaps necessary, to enforce the exercise of a hierarchical control which was more concerned to juridically define the valid than to enlarge the imagination and its awareness of symbolism. There were indeed reasons for this when celebrations were put in question, largely due to faults in priestly life and celebration, but unfortunately these minimally liturgical and excessively juridical attitudes dominated Latin liturgy for too long. The absence of appreciative awareness at the altar, however, did not mean that attention to water and oil and fire, or even to bread, as holy or sacred things disappeared from the popular imagination or from popular ritual practices. From recent times we need only think of the attachment to Lourdes' water or to a less spectacular holy water taken home from churches, or of the distribution of St. Anthony's or St. Joseph's bread, or of the lighting of candles before images of Christ, Mary, and the saints. Officially the church incorporated some of these practices into its ritual books, but often the blessings associated with them took on the color of exorcism. This corresponded to the sense of the precarious which often invaded human existence when people relied on Earth's produce and saw it frequently threatened by greater forces. Knowing how dependent their economy and lifestyle were on these things, people knew in their bones that they needed to be freed from evil and recommended to divine providential care. The mysterious relation of such material elements to human life could not be forgotten, even if liturgies as it were "forgot" them. Sometimes popular practice seemed superstitious. In our day scientific inquiry changes mentalities and ways of dealing with produce and need, but science can either diminish awe or call for attention to a world that remains still little known to humans. In a sense the growth of superstitious fear will disappear only when the elements are restored to liturgy surrounded by awe and reverence within the acclaim of a loving God.

The second reason why we need to attend to things of Earth in worship is allied to people's dependence on Earth and on human benevolence in dealing with Earth's produce, whether natural, agricultural, or mineral. Exploitation of Earth's resource within a profit-motivated global economy deprives people of resources and disturbs the environment in which people live, destroying natural habitats and causing a pollution of the atmosphere with effects that reach out into the cosmos. Eco-justice has to render its dues to both humans and nature, which has been pointed out by many nongovernmental organizations as well as by bishops around the world, by Popes John Paul II and Benedict XVI, and by Patriarch Bartholomew of Constantinople. The churches, East and West, now foster policies of production and distribution that embody a greater sense of the wonder of the cosmos and of humanity's belonging within a vaster creation. In some measure they connect their humanitarian efforts with liturgy and covenant remembrance as did Pope John Paul II in convoking the Jubilee observance of AD 2000 and as is frequently done by Patriarch Bartholemew. While this eco-justice may not be an explicit concern in Gibler's work, her reflections have repercussions on it, for what is always at stake is the way in which the human is connected with Earth and its place within the vastly larger Universe.

The third thing that prompts to fresh sensitivity to earthly and cosmic elements in worship arises from what not only scientists but even ordinary mortals have learned from scientific exploration of the cosmos. Liturgy has always been attentive to the symbols or sacraments which Linda Gibler here explores, attentive both to domestic immediacy and to cosmic totality, as exemplified in Tertullian's praise of water in his treatise on baptism, or by Melito of Sardis as quoted in this book. In turn, Augustine spoke of the four symbols of bread, wine, oil, and water as the four sacraments of the Christian Church: they are domestic and homely, but they also bring the rhythms of creation into dwellings and place them on the table. Generally, however, in the times of these writers this reverence fit into a vision of Divine Providence that ordered all things according to knowable patterns. There is today a new awareness at different levels of the vast reality of which the Earth itself and the humans who dwell on it are a minuscule part, whereas for centuries they were thought of as center of the Universe, and God was seen to be all-seeing from the high tower of medieval imagination, governing everything according to hierarchies inherent to a divine plan. The image of a Creator God may seem threatened by new discoveries, since we have not yet developed the theoretical framework within which to envelop the new knowledge of things that exist and so of a creation that allows for them. Imaginative and symbolic language becomes more important in such a flux, for beyond the rational mind it has ways of expressing awareness and feeling and faith that remain alive and lively. So how can liturgy let these things speak now of themselves, within an expanding sense of nature and cosmos, and still see them within the praise of the creating and saving God?

Dr. Gibler's book responds in some way to all three of the above concerns. She weaves three strands together in the recovery of the symbolism of the elements she has chosen for her study: water, oil, and fire.

Something similar has to be done for bread and wine and plastic arts, but when it is done much may be learned from the approach she has taken. The first concern of the author is to enlarge the story of these elements in the cosmos and the evolution of life on Earth so as to show humanity's enfolding into a much greater story. The invitation and the language are challenging to imagination, feeling, and thought, but this is as it should be. On this foundation Gibler unravels in turn the complexity of biblical stories and of liturgical traditions. As for these stories she has made creative use of the large number of studies more widely known. The originality of her contribution lies in how she develops their place in the cosmic and earthly story and relates the expressions of a faith tradition to this. This responds both to the need to situate ourselves and our liturgies in the vastness of the Universe and to the expanding awe before the mystery of God which discovery elicits, without losing the sense of divine love operative in all of creation and of the love poured out in a particular way on humanity by the sending of the Word Incarnate and of the Spirit. What is provided by more recent discovery can then become integral to the recovery of the better known traditions of Bible and liturgy. A retrieval of symbolic action may be aided when people are more in wonder at the elements themselves and what wonders they evoke. The creation story and hymns to divine Wisdom and to Christ, the firstborn from the dead and lord of creation, sound more wonderful in face of this cosmic story and its convergence with Judeo-Christian story and tradition, as does the recall of the kenotic mystery of incarnation in human flesh.

Gibler, in her own compositions, while drawing quite evidently from liturgical traditions, weaves the sense of cosmos and humanity's connection with cosmos and Earth, sometimes nowadays put under the symbol of Gaia, into her prayer. There may still be an inevitably uneasy fit, for at present, knowledge of the cosmic has more science than story behind it, whereas liturgical prayer needs story. Compositions of the early Roman liturgy incorporated the prevailing social and spiritual sense of Order through their reading of the Creation and Wisdom story, but this seems to us now an uneasy fit to the extent that it promoted a social ordering of hierarchical dominions in all spheres of life. In face of what is particular to our time, Gibler's compositions show a comparable process, for they too are attentive to social murmurings and patterns, raising the question whether one can fit the new perceptions with the old stories and blessings without an uneasy juxtaposition. But maybe that is ever the story of liturgy and of liturgical renewal and even more so when the church is more pluralistic and self-consciously trying things out. The common imagination to which we appeal is lacking, and so artistic exploration is more necessary. It took a long time before early prayers in all liturgical traditions were given fixed and stable form, and that has to be the case today also, even in face of efforts to control such prayer anew.

With all these things in mind, Linda Gibler's work is a valuable read for liturgical scholars and for bishops and any ministers, ordained or otherwise, who have responsibility for liturgical leadership. Beyond such special readers it has much to offer to anyone concerned with the mystery that is being celebrated and unfolded within the rituals of churches, whatever their tradition.

ACKNOWLEDGMENTS

A complete list of those to whom I am grateful as I conclude this book would truly reach the stars and cover the Earth. Even a short list is rather long.

First and always, I am grateful to my Dominican Family: to the Dominican Sisters of Houston, my own congregation, and to the Mission San Jose Dominicans, with whom I lived during much of my writing. I am particularly grateful to Jane, who introduced me to cosmology, and to Ginger, who saw further than most of us.

I am grateful to the students and faculty of the California Institute of Integral Studies; to my dissertation group, Rod, John, Gregory, Jake, and John; and to my readers, Robert McDermott, John Haught; and especially to Brian Swimme, my mentor.

I am grateful to my colleagues at the Oblate School of Theology, especially to Ron Rolheiser, Elaine Brothers, and the Lunch Bunch.

I am grateful to family and friends, especially to Dad, my brother Ed, and to Becky, Debbie, and Joe.

Along with all these people and many more, I am grateful to the other-than-humans who accompanied me, for keeping me grounded and always luring me back to wonder.

At Genesis Farm there is a tradition of gathering around the kitchen table before meals and naming what we are grateful for that day. If I were to stand at that table today and name everyone who has my gratitude as I conclude this book, the food would grow cold before I could count the stars, list the creatures, and name the people without whom I could not have completed this work. Thank you. You are on each page.

INTRODUCTION

The Universe is God-drenched. Every being, form, and particle of the Universe mediates and responds to God's blessing and has something to teach those who listen. Sacramentals in particular have much to tell. *From the Beginning to Baptism* focuses on three sacramentals used in the Catholic celebration of baptism: water, olive oil, and the fire atop a lighted candle. It traces their scientific stories from the Beginning, 13.7 billion years ago when the Universe was first created, through the formation of Earth, to the embodiment of each of these sacramentals within the individual persons celebrating baptism. It then explores the sacred significance of water, oil, and fire as they appear in biblical narratives, in ancient teachings, and then in contemporary baptismal instructions and blessings. Once these stories are told, we explore what they might mean to a person preparing for baptism. What we find is that the integration of the sacramentals' stories provides new insights into the sacramentals themselves, into baptism, and into God, whose blessing they reveal.

This integration of scientific and sacred stories suggests a cosmocentric sacramentality, one that locates human sacramental experience within the context of the Universe. Without diminishing the teaching of the church, this sacramental perspective reveals the intimate connection between the persons celebrating a sacrament and the Earth community, between the moment of the celebration and the history of the Universe from its beginning to today and into the future. In short, a cosmocentric sacramentality is one that fully believes that God is truly present to and in each aspect of creation, that the Universe is God-drenched.

HISTORICAL BACKGROUND

Before we begin the stories of water, oil, and fire, it makes sense to situate this kind of perspective within the Roman Catholic and scientific traditions. *From the Beginning to Baptism* flows from Roman Catholic tradition and contributes to an emerging functional cosmology.[1] We will see that a cosmocentric appreciation of sacraments is rooted in patristic writings and is again supported by contemporary theological developments. Cosmocentric sacramentality is centered in the heritage of Pierre Teilhard de Chardin. It is informed by the scientific story of the Universe with its implications for revitalizing relationships between humans and the Earth community.

Roman Catholic Tradition

To situate this work within the Roman Catholic tradition we turn first to the patristic retrievals by Kilian McDonnell and Paul Palmer and then to the more contemporary insights of Edward Schillebeeckx, Edward Kilmartin, and Kenan Osborne.

Patristic Roots
Patristic theology of the early church provides roots for a cosmocentric approach to sacramentality. Even though the church's relationship to the material world later developed in problematic directions, the notion of sacramentals participating in divinity in their own right was a central aspect of early sacramental experience. Kilian McDonnell's *The Baptism of Jesus in the Jordan* and Paul Palmer's *Sacraments and Worship* provide a glimpse into sacramental experience within the nascent church. McDonnell assembles early documents that refer to baptism and the catechesis of new initiates. Palmer has collected liturgical rites from the first to the twentieth century. From different starting points these works combine to form a compelling, grounding view of the early church's experience of the world.

In *The Baptism of Jesus in the Jordan*,[2] Kilian McDonnell retrieves the cosmic significance of the baptism of Jesus and demonstrates that it

1. As will become clear below, Thomas Berry uses the term "functional cosmology" to indicate a worldview that will "provide the mystique needed" for integral Earth-human relationships. Thomas Berry, *The Dream of the Earth* (San Francisco: Sierra Club Books, 1988), 66, 90–91.

2. Kilian McDonnell, *The Baptism of Jesus in the Jordan: The Trinitarian and Cosmic Order of Salvation* (Collegeville, MN: Liturgical Press, 1996).

was a major mystery in the life of the early church.[3] Within this work he discusses the cosmic nature of the three sacramentals of water, oil, and fire, beginning with the three cosmic understandings of water in Jesus' baptism: universal baptism, new creation, and cosmic consecration. Concerning the oil used to anoint in baptism, McDonnell draws from the two anointings described by Irenaeus and then discusses anointing in rituals of naming and acknowledgment. McDonnell considers the fire of the lighted candle received at baptism in terms of both flame and light. I discuss each of these insights into cosmic significance in detail in subsequent chapters. McDonnell stresses that the role of the cosmos in the baptism of Jesus was more than symbolic to members of the early church. The patristic tradition experienced natural elements as part of the witness of the created Universe to the baptism and ministry of Jesus. For the early church water, oil, and fire participated in this mediating, revelatory ministry. Water cleansed; oil rejoiced; fire transformed.

In *Sacraments and Worship* Paul Palmer gathers the extant liturgies, writings, canons, as well as decrees of ecumenical councils that relate to sacraments.[4] Although he traces the development of sacramental understanding through Pope Pius XII (to 1947), he focuses primarily on documents from the first through the eighth centuries. Since then the rites of the church have been relatively stable, such that the Gelasian Sacramentary, composed in the sixth century, would be strikingly familiar to contemporary Catholics.

Showing the importance of the sacramentals for the early church, Palmer writes in his introduction:

> Underlying early Christian worship is the principle that matter is good, that material things, such as water and oil, wheat and wine, are susceptible of the divine influence, and even capable of acting as the instrument or vehicle of the Holy Spirit in the transformation of the human spirit. . . . [which is] an immediate corollary of the Incarnation wherein the "Word became flesh." . . . Not only are material things the medium by which God approaches man, external rites and ceremonies are the medium by which man approaches God.[5]

---

3. Ibid., x.

4. Paul F. Palmer, ed., *Sacraments and Worship: Liturgy and Doctrinal Development of Baptism, Confirmation, and the Eucharist*, vol. 1, Sources of Christian Theology (Westminster, MD: Newman Press, 1955).

5. Ibid., vii.

Like McDonnell, Palmer traces the uses and meanings of the sacramentals of water, oil, and fire from their earliest use in Christian baptism, demonstrating that rich cosmological understandings of the sacramentals are explicit in the early texts of the church. Although this appreciation has largely been lost in modern practice, patristic tradition provides fertile ground for the retrieval and development of a cosmocentric sacramentality. Although medieval theology is concerned with the metaphysics of matter, it does not consider the specifics of particular sacramentals. For this reason we move directly to contemporary sacramental theology.

Contemporary Theological Development

Edward Schillebeeckx, Edward Kilmartin, and Kenan Osborne each extend the boundaries of thought about sacraments away from the narrow interpretation inherited from the Council of Trent in the direction of greater cosmic inclusiveness. Although these theologians do not consider the history or nature of sacramentals themselves, they do provide fertile ground for that development. Following the inquiries of Dom Odo Casel, and aligned with Karl Rahner,[6] Edward Schillebeeckx expands the use of sacrament beyond the seven ritual sacraments prescribed by Trent to include the notion of Jesus as the primordial sacrament.[7] According to Schillebeeckx, Jesus was the sacrament out of which all other sacraments flow because of the completeness of Jesus' human response to God and God's perfect embrace of Jesus' humanity. Schillebeeckx further elaborates that the church is a foundational sacrament because it extends Jesus' body in time. The church is Jesus' presence to the world now, and its members are the body of the church. However, Schillebeeckx does not limit the body of Christ to the Roman Catholic Church or even to the Christian churches. He holds that people of every faith constitute the body of Christ. In his work, which the Second Vatican Council embraced, the notion of sacrament moves beyond its ritual meaning. The meaning of sacrament extends to the person of Jesus, flows into the church as the body of Christ, and includes the entire human community of believers in any faith.

6. See especially "The Sacramental Life" in Karl Rahner, *Foundations of Christian Faith: An Introduction to the Idea of Christianity* (New York: Seabury Press, 1978), 411–30.

7. Edward Schillebeeckx, *Christ the Sacrament of the Encounter with God* (New York: Sheed and Ward, 1963).

Later theologians such as Edward Kilmartin and Kenan Osborne extend this meaning of sacrament from people of faith to the cosmos itself. Kilmartin holds that an appreciation of nature must be at the heart of a cosmic sacramentality.[8] For Osborne every cloud is a potential sacramental and every natural object conveys God's blessing.[9] It is not until a human responds, however, that the blessing becomes sacramental. Both Kilmartin and Osborne point to a sacramentality of the cosmos but neither develops the concept or explores what such an extension might mean for an understanding of sacramentals.

Schillebeeckx, Kilmartin, and Osborne suggest two points of departure for a cosmocentric sacramentality. The first is that all things are potential sacramentals. I argue that the better we know these sacramental beings, the better we know God. The second point of departure is the idea that all beings respond to God's blessing. Ritual sacraments are a continuation of the blessing and response that began at the birth of the Universe. All creation is a potential sacramental, and every being in creation has the potential to respond sacramentally to God's blessing.

FUNCTIONAL COSMOLOGY

The sacramental vibrancy of creation is a central aspect of a functional cosmology. To situate this work within this lineage we turn first to Pierre Teilhard de Chardin and then to Thomas Berry, Brian Swimme, and John Haught.

Pierre Teilhard de Chardin knew Earth as sacramental. He saw everything as shining with the indwelling spirit of Jesus. His relationship with God immanent in matter was eucharistic. In his "Mass on the World," Teilhard relates the experience of offering Mass without the usual sacramentals of chalice, paten, wine, or bread. In place of these elements he offered the whole of creation to God for transubstantiation. He writes:

> Over every living thing which is to spring up, to grow, to flower, to ripen during this day say again the words: This is my Body. And over every

---

8. Edward J. Kilmartin, "Theology of the Sacraments: Toward a New Understanding of the Chief Rites of the Church of Jesus Christ," in *Alternative Futures for Worship*, vol. 1, ed. Regis J. Duffy, 123–75 (Collegeville, MN: Liturgical Press, 1987).

9. Kenan B. Osborne, *Christian Sacraments in a Postmodern World: A Theology for the Third Millennium* (New York: Paulist Press, 1999).

death-force which waits in readiness to corrode, to wither, to cut down, speak again your commanding words which express the supreme mystery of faith: This is my blood.[10]

In this prayer Teilhard sees the entire world, all its people, forces, being, and matter as transformed into the body and blood of Jesus. He tells us that "at the touch of the supersubstantial Word, the immense host which is the universe is made flesh."[11] Through God's incarnation, "all matter is henceforth incarnate."[12] This sacramental awareness of the indwelling of divinity in all matter is the basis of Teilhard's religious experience. Speaking to God, he says: "As for me, if I could not believe that your real Presence animates and makes tractable and enkindles even the very least of the energies which invade me or brush past me, would I not die of cold?"[13] His effort to see everything around him as the body and blood of the Word, shining from every element and event, required a constant faith. If his faith should falter, the light would recede and the world would again seem darkened. Teilhard's desire not to lose sight of the presence of the Word in matter led him to pray for faith to discover and sense God in every creature.

Seeking a sacramental vision of the infusion of God into matter was Teilhard's fundamental way of relating to God and experiencing the world. Again addressing God, he says:

> For me, my God, all joy and all achievement, the very purpose of my being and all my love of life, all depend on this basic vision of the union between yourself and the universe. . . . I have no desire, I have no ability, to proclaim anything except the innumerable prolongations of your incarnate Being in the world of matter; I can preach only the mystery of your flesh, you the Soul shining forth through all that surrounds us.[14]

Teilhard's God-drenched vision of matter pervades his spiritual as well as his scientific writings. His spiritual conception of matter provides the foundation through which those who were influenced by him see matter as more than soulless or mechanical. Thanks to Teilhard's profound vision

10. Pierre Teilhard de Chardin, "Mass on the World," in idem, *The Heart of Matter* (New York: Harcourt Brace Jovanovich, 1978), 123.

11. Ibid., 24.

12. Ibid.

13. Ibid., 25.

14. Ibid., 36–37.

and poetic writing, his love of God in matter influenced Thomas Berry, who made it the basis for the lineage of functional cosmology.

Sharing Teilhard's experience of the world, cultural historian Thomas Berry recognizes the ways in which the destruction inflicted on Earth by Western civilization is a consequence of the forgotten integral relationship with the Earth community. In *The Dream of the Earth*, a book that has become a touchstone for cosmologically minded people, Berry offers a critique of this disenchanted view of the Universe and stresses the need for a functional cosmology that can guide and discipline our human use of knowledge, skill, and resources for the benefit of the entire Earth community.[15]

In "Christianity and the American Experience," an essay in *The Dream of the Earth*, Berry points to four ways in which Christianity has contributed to a worldview in which nonhuman nature is seen as spiritually valueless. First, Christianity typically identifies the divine as separated from the natural world. Berry says that by placing God outside creation "we negate the natural world as the locus for the meeting of the divine and the human."[16] The divine is precluded from an intimate relationship with the natural world. A second and related problem is the Christian "insistence that the human is a spiritual being with an eternal destiny which is beyond that of the members of the created world," thereby orphaning humans from nature.[17] Third, the Cartesian conception of nature deprived nonhuman beings of inner life. Berry writes: "The concept of crass matter emerged as mere extension, capable only of externally manipulated and mechanistic activity. We entered into a mechanistic phase in our thinking and in our basic norms of reality and value."[18]

The fourth way Christianity has contributed to a disenchanted worldview is the persistent belief that human history is progressing toward a millennial age. Berry says: "While the millennium was originally considered as a spiritual condition to be brought about infallibly by a divine providence, it was later interpreted simply as an age of human fulfillment to be brought about by human skill in exploiting the resources of the earth."[19]

15. Thomas Berry, *The Dream of the Earth* (San Francisco: Sierra Club Books, 1988).
16. Ibid., 113.
17. Ibid.
18. Ibid., 114.
19. Ibid.

These four aspects of Western Christianity facilitate a disenchanted view of the world. God is experienced as separate from nature. The uniqueness of the human soul leaves nature soulless and distant from humans. This disenchantment, paired with a millennial promise, leaves humans to build their future out of the "crass" materials of nature. Within this disenchanted worldview, everything awaits transformation by divine will and human work; nothing has significance unless it is transformed to meet human needs. As a result, the natural world has become emptied of its "unique modes of divine presence," reduced in its ability to elicit spiritual response and diminished in its beauty.[20]

This worldview helped produce a technology that nature cannot withstand. Because the sacredness of Earth was disregarded, Earth's resources are used almost exclusively for shortsighted human gain, turning humanity into an unchecked planetary force with little regard for ecological consequences. Berry reminds us: "We now begin to realize, however, that the planet Earth will not long endure being despised or ignored in its more integral being, whether by scientists, technologists, or saints; nor will it submit forever to the abuse it has had to endure."[21]

Berry suggests that a new ecological age is dawning that will require the construction of a new spiritual context that includes the Universe and the Earth community. This spirituality must be grounded in a deeply participatory experience of the Universe, and particularly the Earth as the primary locus of divine presence, making it the primary educator, healer, commercial establishment, and lawgiver. Moreover, this new spirituality must be based on the characteristics of Earth itself, by which he means that it must honor the uniqueness of each individual as well as the bondedness of each being with every other being in the Universe. Berry insists that

> the greatest single need at the present is the completion of the story, as told in its physical dimensions by science, by the more integral accounts that include the numinous and consciousness dimensions of the emergent universe from its primordial moment. Once that is done, a meaningful universe, a functional cosmology, is available as a foundation for the range of human activities in the ecological age.[22]

20. Ibid., 115.
21. Ibid., 119.
22. Ibid., 120.

Because of the richness of what we are learning about the Universe through the revelations of science and emerging ecological consciousness, "a new vision and a new vigor are available to Christian tradition."[23] While Teilhard provides a sweeping vision of a numinous world, Berry adjusts the focus of this vision to develop an Earth-centered spirituality and adds a critique of the human social institutions responsible for ecological degradation. Berry sees the way into a new ecological era through the creation of a functional cosmology based on knowledge of the Universe as an integral community.

In *The Universe Story*, Brian Swimme and Thomas Berry reinfuse deep meaning into the story of the Universe, reveal its cosmic integrative principles, and provide a vision for the "Ecozoic Era."[24] Swimme and Berry celebrate the story of the Universe, beginning with the Flaring Forth and continuing through the birth of stars, galaxies, and planets to the formation of Earth and the emergence of life. In this book they trace human life from its tribal beginnings through the classical and medieval civilizations to modern industrial society, situating this epic story within a critique of the effect of industrial society on the Earth community. Swimme and Berry offer this story as a foundation for the development of a functional cosmology, which would "enable the human community to become present to the larger Earth community in a mutually enhancing manner."[25]

Throughout their telling of the cosmogenetic story of the Universe and how it emerges, Swimme and Berry provide a vision of the Ecozoic Era. The central theme of the Ecozoic Era is the Universe as a "communion of subjects rather than a collection of objects."[26] Through such communion the damage inflicted on the planet will begin to heal as humans enter into mutually enhancing relationships with members of the Earth community. Through this deeper intimacy humans will come to understand that they share a common destiny with all the beings of the Earth community. To transition into this Ecozoic Era, Swimme and Berry recommend that the human professions all must realize that their prototype and their primary—first and foundational—resource is the integral functioning of the Earth community. This places Earth at the center and source of every

23. Ibid., 122.

24. Brian Swimme and Thomas Berry, *The Universe Story: From the Primordial Flaring Forth to the Ecozoic Era—a Celebration of the Unfolding of the Cosmos* (San Francisco: HarperSanFrancisco, 1992).

25. Ibid., 3.

26. Ibid., 243.

profession. They continue: "The natural world itself is the primary economic reality, the primary educator, the primary governance, the primary technologist, the primary healer, the primary presence of the sacred, the primary moral value."[27] In order to see Earth as primary we must "awaken a consciousness of the sacred dimension of the Earth." Swimme and Berry advise the religious professions that their basic concern must be to "preserve the natural world as the primary revelation of the divine." The primary sacred community is the Universe.

In *The Promise of Nature*, John Haught asks "whether the religions of the world, particularly Christianity, have the resources to contribute anything of substance to the resolution of our current ecological predicament."[28] After an explication of the essential parts of an "ecologically wholesome" religion, Haught concludes: "the survival and flourishing of the earth is dependent on the survival and flourishing of religion," not any religion, but one that is sacramentally balanced and grounded in eschatological hope.

Haught suggests four distinct aspects of an ecologically wholesome religion—sacramental, mystical, silent, and active:

> The sacramental way invites us to enjoy the natural world in a spirit of gratitude for the gift that it is. The mystical way, on the other hand, exhorts us to relativize nature, that is, to keep it in perspective. The way of silence, as exemplified by Buddhism or the Jewish Sabbath, ask us simply to let the world be itself, lest in our arrogance we end up reducing it to what corresponds only to the human will. The *active* component of religion, however, persuades us to change the world. And herein there seems to lie a problem, environmentally speaking.[29]

Haught hastens to say that the activist impulse of biblical religion "is culpable only where it has lost touch with the sacramental, mystical and silent aspects that are also essential to biblical religion."[30] He tells us that the most important thing a religion can do to meet the ecological crisis is to "make sure that its mystical, silent and active tendencies always remain very close to the sacramental."[31]

27. Ibid., 255.
28. John Haught, *The Promise of Nature: Ecology and Cosmic Purpose* (New York: Paulist Press, 1993), 2.
29. Ibid., 83.
30. Ibid., 84.
31. Ibid., 87.

A sacramental religion uses concrete symbols, usually from nature, to talk about the sacred, and relies upon these symbols to reveal its ineffable mystery. Haught tells us that "a sacramental vision makes nature, at least in a fragmentary way, transparent to divinity."[32] Because it is capable of mediating the hidden mystery of the divine, nature is intrinsically valuable. With value returned to nature, sacramentalism can ground an ecological ethic because the integrity of the symbols must be maintained if they are to remain transparent to mystery. To hold a sacramental view of the world it is necessary to advocate "the welfare and intrinsic value of our natural environment."[33] When a religion loses touch with its sacramental heritage it risks insensitivity to the natural world. But is sacramentality enough? Haught replies in the negative:

> A purely sacramental or creation-centered theology of nature cannot easily accommodate the shadow side of nature. By focusing on ecological harmony, it expects us to see every present state of nature as an epiphany of God. This is a projection which neither our religion nor the natural world can bear . . . A sacramental theology is all by itself unable to ac-commodate the fact of nature's fragility.[34]

To address the problem of nature's fragility, Haught turns to the bib-lical mandate of hope in future fulfillment. He says: "The perspective of hope allows us to be realistic about what nature is. We do not have to cover up its cruelty. We can accept the fact that the cosmos is not a paradise but only the promise thereof."[35] Nature is unfinished. Like the entire cosmos, nature is "an adventurous journey toward the complexity and beauty of a future perfection."[36] Billions of years before humanity emerged, the cosmos was already "seeded with promise." The promise we see in nature now is an unfolding of the same promise and "carries with it the whole universe's yearning for its future."[37] Hope for the future is embedded within the emerging story of the Universe; Christianity will be carried into the fulfillment it hopes for, companioned by nature. All members of the Earth community share the same journey. Haught con-

32. Ibid., 78.
33. Ibid., 77.
34. Ibid., 111–12.
35. Ibid., 111.
36. Ibid., 110.
37. Ibid., 109.

cludes: "What makes nature deserve our care is not that it is divine but that it is pregnant with a mysterious future."[38]

In summary, Thomas Berry and Brian Swimme provide an Earth-centered critique of industrial society and build the foundation for a functional cosmology. Through the telling of the story of the Universe and the explanation of its cosmogenetic principles, they also situate humanity within the Universe and Earth community and call on all professions to re-vision their work, using Earth as the primary model. Within this context, they advise that moving into an Ecozoic Era requires an awareness of the sacredness of Earth so that humans can learn to live in mutually enhancing relationships with the Earth community. John Haught takes up the problem of the role of religion in moving into the future by asking why religion should care about nature. He offers a sacramental-eschatological theology that sees nature as promise. The Universe was seeded with promise from its beginnings and this promise continues to unfold in Christianity's yearning for future fulfillment. Religion should care about nature because it mirrors the divine and because it holds the promise of the future.

The cosmocentric sacramentality I develop here is grounded in Catholic tradition and continues the lineage of functional cosmology. Patristic instructions to catechumens and the blessings used during the rites of baptism reveal the deep participation of the created world in sacramentality. In the early church all aspects of creation were experienced as participants in manifesting and responding to divine blessing. Contemporary Catholic theology extends the meaning of sacraments from seven ritual moments to the Catholic Church itself and then to all people. These extensions invite the additional inclusion of other-than-humans in sacramental responsiveness. Working from a different direction, a functional cosmology begins with the sacredness of the cosmos and the Earth community and then asks how religious institutions participate within that sacredness. Situated within both of these traditions, this book develops a cosmocentric sacramentality through the integration of the cosmological and sacramental histories of water, oil, and fire.

A spirituality of learning from sacramentals carries sacred meaning from ritual celebration into daily practice. An intimate understanding of the cosmic and sacred meaning of a sacramental used in baptism enables that sacramental to carry its meaning into the homes and lives of baptismal participants. When we begin to believe that natural objects have a history

38. Ibid., 110.

of participating in blessing and response, we will recall their sacredness more frequently when we encounter them and become less likely to behave in ways that endanger them and the Earth community.

CONTENTS

From the Beginning to Baptism is presented in four chapters following this introduction and background. The next three chapters have parallel structures, each focusing on one of the sacramentals of baptism: water, oil, and fire, respectively. Each of these chapters begins with a prayer that arose from my reflection on the sacramental. The prayer is threaded through the chapter as a means to hold the sacred center of this work. Each chapter first presents the natural history of the sacramental and traces its story from the Beginning, through the formation of Earth, into the body of a person participating in baptism.

After this story is told, the chapter continues with the sacred story of the sacramental. This section of the chapter begins by tracing the history of the sacramental in Scripture from its Old Testament roots through the New Testament. Then, using blessings and instructions to catechumens, the story of the sacramental is traced through the first centuries of the early church and continues with the current blessings and prayers and the instructions in the Rite of Christian Initiation for Adults[39] and in the *Catechism of the Catholic Church.*[40]

The third section of each of the next three chapters offers a cosmocentric integration of the natural history and sacred stories of the sacramental, including an investigation of the sacramental using Pierre Teilhard de Chardin's thresholds of development. In *The Human Phenomenon,*[41] Teilhard described four stages in Earth's development: pre-life, life, thought, and superlife. The pre-life stage begins with the formation of matter and energy at the Beginning and continues until Earth crosses the threshold into life. The life stage begins with the formation of the first

---

39. *The Rites of the Catholic Church*, vol. 1 (Collegeville, MN: Liturgical Press, 1990).

40. *Catechism of the Catholic Church*, Revised in Accordance with the Official Latin Text Promulgated by Pope John Paul II, 2nd ed. (Washington, DC: United States Catholic Conference, 1997).

41. Pierre Teilhard de Chardin, *The Human Phenomenon*, trans. Sarah Appleton-Weber (Portland, OR: Sussex Academic Press, 2003).

life and continues until Earth crosses the threshold into thought. For Teilhard this threshold is crossed only when self-reflective consciousness emerges in humans. This stage includes the notion of noosphere—the sphere of human thought that Teilhard envisioned encircling the Earth. The threshold into superlife is crossed as this layer of thought thickens and condenses as the number of thinking beings increases. As it does, Teilhard says, "thanks to the tremendous biological event that the discovery of electromagnetic waves represents, each individual from now on is simultaneously present (actively and passively) to the whole of the seas and continents—coextensive with the Earth."[42]

Although Teilhard is clear that the superlife stage of Earth does not belong to a preferred race or elite group of people, he limits participation in it to humans.[43] In contrast to Teilhard and following the inclinations of a functional cosmology, I include the Universe and Earth community in a cosmocentric integration of the superlife phase. As John Haught tells us, "it is incongruous to think of our own destiny . . . as though the whole universe did not somehow share in this same destiny, hope, and promise."[44] After a cosmocentric investigation of the sacramental in light of Teilhard's thresholds for Earth's development, each chapter concludes with a reflection from the perspective of a person who has learned the stories of the sacramental in preparation for baptism.

The concluding chapter of *From the Beginning to Baptism* then draws together the information about the sacramentals from the previous three chapters and applies it to an appreciation of baptism and sacramentality in general. After key points from the integration of the scientific and sacred stories are gathered, Teilhard's developmental thresholds are applied to the ritual of baptism and a cosmocentric view of baptism is presented. Next, these cosmocentric insights about baptism are applied to the other six ritual sacraments of the Catholic Church and, finally, extended to a sacramentality that embraces the Universe and draws from our hearts.

42. Ibid., 167–70.
43. Ibid., 168.
44. Haught, *The Promise of Nature*, 127.

Chapter One

WATER

A Blessing of Water

Blessed are you, Ever-Present God,
Creator of the Universe,
Through you we have the gift of water for baptism.

Water that formed in the remnants of ancient stars
and brought our Day Star to birth.
Water that cooled the nascent Earth.
Rising from deep within and carried by comets,
your water drenched our young planet
and covered it in oceans.
Water that birthed the first life on Earth
and each life thereafter
Water that fills and flows within every living being.

This water of Stars, Earth, and Life you give
to bring us into fullness of life in you.
This is the water over which your Spirit hovered at the Beginning,
the water that cleansed the Earth in Noah's day,
through which the Israelites passed unharmed
in Moses' day,
and in which Jesus was baptized.

This is the water Jesus calmed,
  the water he turned into wine in Cana,
  and that flowed from his side on Calvary.

Ever-Present God, your Spirit continuously moves within water.
  Enliven the water in this font and in us
  so we may remember that all water flows
  with your holy presence.

Blessed are you, Ever-Present God,
  Creator of the Universe,
  Through you we have the gift of water for baptism.[1]

Creation is water-drenched. All living beings on Earth are born of water—in oceans or ponds, within eggs, seeds, or wombs. In even the most arid climates on Earth, all living beings rely on water. Water surrounds and fills the cells of every living thing. It is the circulation of water throughout a being that sustains its life. Even nonliving beings are shaped by water. As we shall see, water cools stars and planets. Mountains are eroded and valleys molded by water's persistent presence. Without water there is no life; there are no stars, no living planets, no clouds, no mountains, no prairies, and no children of any species.

Water is sacred. Our Bibles overflow with stories of water. The significance of water in baptism is told most dramatically in the stories of creation, the great flood, the crossing of the Red Sea and the Jordan River, and in Jesus' own baptism. Water's sacredness has been acknowledged in the Christian mysteries since the earliest days of the church. Baptismal fonts or pools are prominent in most churches, and water is placed near church doors so that the faithful walk past it every time they enter a church.[2] Especially at Easter, water is sprinkled on the congregation as a blessing. It is mixed with wine at each eucharistic celebration. Few Catholic celebrations occur without the presence of water.

The prayer that begins this chapter is a blessing inspired by my reflections on scientific and sacred stories of water. It is modeled on the blessing prayed during the Easter Vigil, which recalls water's participation in

1. All prayers that introduce chapters are the author's.
2. This water is removed for the forty days of Lent to recall the Israelites' forty years in the desert. Through water's absence, the entire season of Lent becomes a time of waiting for passage into new life.

salvation history, and blends in some of the wonders of the natural history of water. Both the Easter prayer and this prayer praise God for the gift of water, acknowledge the gift by telling the stories of water, and ask God's Spirit to be present through water once again. We read in Genesis that water was central to Earth's creation. Now, through the revelations of science, we know that water itself emerged billions of years earlier through forces initiated in the early Universe and continued in stars. The natural history in this new prayer expresses water's story from the Beginning, 13.7 billion years ago, and reminds us that water has flowed with God's blessing since it first condensed amid clouds of stardust. This chapter is an explication of this scientific/sacred blessing of water.

This explication occurs in three sections: "The Natural History of Water," "The Sacramental Story of Water," and "Integrating the Stories of Water." The natural history tells of the creation of water and its continuing role in creating and sustaining life. The sacramental story traces the use of water in the Catholic rite of baptism from its biblical beginning to the present. After navigating these two streams of the history of water we arrive at the confluence of the natural history and the sacramental stories of water in its renewed significance for baptism.

THE NATURAL HISTORY OF WATER

Water's Birth

> Blessed are you, Gracious God,
>   Creator of the Universe,
>   Through you we have the gift of water for baptism.
> Water that formed in the remnants of ancient stars
>   and brought our Day Star to birth.

Hydrogen

The story of water—indeed, the story of everything in the Universe —begins with hydrogen. In the first fractions of a second after the Beginning, tiny particles of matter formed.[3] These particles, or protons, were

---

3. For detailed accounts of the early Universe see Philip Ball, *Life's Matrix: A Biography of Water* (Berkeley: University of California Press, 2001); Armand Delsemme, *Our Cosmic Origins: From the Big Bang to the Emergence of Life and Intelligence* (Cambridge: Cambridge University Press, 1998); Roger A. Freedman and William J.

hydrogen nuclei. The newborn Universe was so hot and dense that for a brief flash of time particles collided so fiercely that most of them were transformed into energy. The Universe quickly expanded and cooled. When the Universe was just one millionth of a second old, the annihilation slowed down; only one billionth of the original particles remained. These surviving bits of matter are the hydrogen nuclei out of which all other matter formed. For the next fifteen minutes, as the Universe continued to expand and cool, when hydrogen nuclei collided they no longer turned into energy but rather fused together to form heavier nuclei of helium, beryllium, and lithium. Soon, as the Universe continued to cool, hydrogen nuclei no longer collided with enough energy to fuse into larger nuclei. When the Universe was only fifteen minutes old, it stopped complexifying.

Three hundred and eighty thousand years later the story of creation entered a new phase with the creation of atoms. By then the Universe had cooled to the point (3000 K) that the positively charged nuclei were able to attract and hold on to negatively charged electrons. As the nuclei bonded with electrons and gained a stable, neutral charge, atoms of hydrogen, helium, and the lightest elements formed. For millions of years these atoms tumbled in the chaos of space. Water's story would have been over before it began if it were not for the surprise of stars.

Oxygen

Slowly, gravity spun this tumble of atoms into webs that spanned the Universe. As the Universe continued to expand, these webs of atoms fractured and folded into dense clusters. Over millions of years the clusters grew larger and their gravitational attraction became greater, drawing even more atoms together. Clusters of atoms grew large enough to compress under their own weight. As they did, they became denser and their centers became hot. This increased heat in their cores radiated outward and caused some clusters simply to dissipate. In others the force of gravity overtook the heat-evoked urge to separate, and these clouds collapsed into themselves, reaching temperatures close to those of the early Universe. In the cores of these hot clouds, atoms lost hold of their electrons, returning them to nuclei. Then, in the largest and hottest clouds, the temperature

---

Kaufmann, *Universe*, 6th ed. (New York: W. H. Freeman and Company, 2002); Joseph Silk, *The Big Bang*, 3d ed. (New York: W. H. Freeman and Company, 2001); Brian Swimme and Thomas Berry, *The Universe Story: From the Primordial Flaring Forth to the Ecozoic Era—a Celebration of the Unfolding of the Cosmos* (San Francisco: HarperSanFrancisco, 1992).

and pressure became so intense that the newly freed nuclei of hydrogen fused together. The energy released by this nuclear fusion ignited the clouds into massive stars.

Within these primal stars the creativity that lay dormant in the Universe once again awakened.[4] Hydrogen nuclei pressed together in the cores of stars first fused into helium. Then, as the stellar centers grew denser and temperatures increased, helium fused into carbon. Carbon, in turn, fused with the remaining helium and formed oxygen—the second element of water. Although most of the stars' oxygen merged into ever-larger nuclei, some of the oxygen escaped the pressure of the stellar cores and reached the cooler edges of their stars. In this calmer environment they were able to bond with electrons and, hundreds of millions of years after the Beginning, the first oxygen atoms formed. In all stars creativity eventually stops. While large stars explode in supernova splendor and small stars die quietly as planetary nebulas, all stars over twice the size of our Sun create oxygen atoms and upon their death release them into space where they encounter waiting hydrogen.

Water

Hydrogen and oxygen finally met in the folds of stellar remnants. Here they tumbled together, not with the force that created new elements, but with enough energy to hold them together and form molecules. Finally, millions of years after the Beginning, water flowed into the Universe, and with it came new powers of creativity.[5]

Water and Creativity

> *Blessed are you, Gracious God,*
> *Creator of the Universe,*
> *Through you we have the gift of water for baptism.*
> *Water that cooled the nascent Earth.*
> *Rising from deep within and carried by comets,*
> *your water drenched our young planet*
> *and covered it in oceans.*

4. For detailed accounts of stellar life cycles see Delsemme, *Our Cosmic Origins;* Freedman and Kaufmann, *Universe;* Swimme and Berry, *The Universe Story*.

5. For more on the origin of water, see chap. 4 in West Marrin, *Universal Water: The Ancient Wisdom and Scientific Theory of Water* (Makawao, Maui, HI: Inner Ocean Publishing, Inc., 2002).

Star Formation

The creativity that flowed into the Universe with water began to express itself almost immediately by assisting the birth of new stars. When the first stars died, their remnants were tossed throughout the Universe. In the turbulence of space, the stellar debris was gathered again by the attraction of gravity and formed into clouds of gas and dust. As with the first stars, gravitational embrace pulled the cloud together while heat from the increased pressure threatened to tear the cloud apart. However, unlike the first time, these stellar clouds contained water vapor with its capacious ability to absorb heat. With the presence of water the outward urge of heat was tempered and gravitational collapse more easily pressed clouds into stars.

Star-birthing regions of space generally have high concentrations of water. In the Orion Cloud complex, water is present at five hundred parts per million. That "small" region of the night sky hidden in Orion's sword contains enough water to fill Earth's oceans ten million times!

Water molecules that assist in a star's birth enjoy two fates. The intensity of stellar heat breaks some water molecules into their component atoms. These atoms are thrown back into space where they may bond again. Other water molecules cling to the dust grains of the collapsing cloud. These water-coated granules either fall into the new star or join the rings of matter that form the star's satellites. In the birth of our Sun the water in these rings eventually became part of the planets, moons, and comets of our Solar System.

Water in the Solar System

Water molecules in our early Solar System had several different fates, determined primarily by their proximity to the Sun. Water is or was present in each of the satellites in the Solar System.[6] These celestial bodies differ greatly in water content. Mercury is one of the few bodies in the Solar System that shows no evidence of water. It is likely that since Mercury formed so close to the Sun its water vaporized, either while it formed or soon thereafter. Venus has a trace of water vapor remaining in its atmosphere, which is slowly being lost to space through the process of photodegeneration, whereby the Sun's energy splits water into hydrogen and oxygen atoms. The freed oxygen atoms remain held by Venus' gravity but the lighter hydrogen atoms float into space. This constant loss of water suggests that Venus was

---

6. For detailed accounts of water in our Solar System see Part II in Freedman and Kaufmann, *Universe*; and chap. 4 in Ball, *Life's Matrix*.

once very wet and perhaps even had liquid surface water. Mars, in contrast to Venus, has water frozen in the red dust particles that cover most of its surface. It also has polar ice made mostly from water and carbon dioxide.

The large gaseous planets, Jupiter and Saturn, have water vapor in their atmospheres and on some of their moons. Jupiter's moons Ganymede and Callisto are rocky cores encased in ice. Europa has an icy surface that shows evidence of a liquid mantle within. Both Europa and Callisto have magnetic fields, which suggest that they have a conductive liquid layer, such as a briny ocean. Io shows no sign of water. It is likely that the gravitation exerted by Jupiter on Io, its closest moon, stripped away any water before it had a chance to collect on the lunar surface. Saturn's moons are also covered with ice. Titan's surface reveals "rocks" made of ice and may have a surface layer of ice six hundred miles thick. The densities of Mimas, Tethys, and Rhea suggest they might be solid ice.

The outer Solar System also contains water. Uranus and Neptune both have extensive inner mantles made of ice mixed with frozen methane and ammonia. Pluto, a dwarf planet in the Kuiper Belt, is a dusty snowball. Beyond the Kuiper Belt with its snowy planetesimals, the Oort Cloud holds comets that are relics of the formation of the Solar System. On average comets are 60 percent ice. When they sweep past the sun their tails release tons of water vapor each second.

Amazingly, even the Sun contains water. Study of the Sun's light reveals water on the surface of the Sun.[7] The water is found in sunspots, which, at temperatures of less than 3500 K, are the coolest regions of the Sun. This "hot water" is also seen in other stars such as Betelgeuse and Antares.

Closer to home, Earth is saturated with water and, unlike on other planets, here it is present in all three of its states. Water in its vaporous state permeates the atmosphere. Liquid water forms the clouds of the atmosphere, falls as rain, and covers most of Earth's surface with oceans. Frozen water covers the highest mountaintops, forms polar caps, and falls as snow and sleet in cold climates.

Formation of Earth

Like other rocky planets, Earth formed through collisions.[8] Particles left over from the formation of the Sun settled into concentric rings

7. Ball, *Life's Matrix*, 110–11.

8. For more on the formation of Earth see chap. 5 in Swimme and Berry, *The Universe Story*; and chap. 3 in Peter D. Ward and Donald Brownlee, *Rare Earth: Why Complex Life Is Uncommon in the Universe* (New York: Copernicus, 2000).

around it. The particles destined to become Earth collided, forming ever larger masses until the material in the ring coalesced into a planet. Initially Earth was quite hot; collisions continued as meteors crashed into Earth. Each new impact created a wave of heat that kept Earth from cooling and brought more material to the planet. Some of these impacts were from the icy comets of the Oort Cloud. These cometary impacts carried large quantities of the water that became part of Earth.

Eventually the rate of the collisions slowed and the molten mix of the planet began to settle. Heavier elements sifted toward the center of the planet, forming its iron core. Lighter elements squeezed and floated toward the surface, forming a brittle crust. The gases and water vapor held by Earth's gravity slowly formed the atmosphere. As with its role in star formation, water vapor accelerated Earth's cooling by absorbing heat, which helped the atmosphere to stabilize.

When Earth was just half a billion years old the water vapor in the atmosphere cooled sufficiently to condense into raindrops. As the rain fell, Earth was sheathed by a shallow ocean.[9] The rain and the ocean cooled the surface magma, which slowly began to form dry land. The early ocean was a murky mix of water, dissolved gases, and minerals. Water's extra-ordinary capacity as a solvent drew minerals out of the ocean floor while streams washed minerals back into the ocean from the newly formed rock crust. This fecund mix of all the elements born of stars settled into the milky matrix of the ocean womb, preparing it to generate life. After being formed by stars and assisting in their birth, water was ready to midwife life on Earth.

Water and Life

> *Blessed are you, Gracious God,*
> *Creator of the Universe,*
> *Through you we have the gift of water for baptism.*
> *Water that birthed the first life on Earth*
> *And each life thereafter*
> *Water that fills and flows within every living being*

---

9. For more on the origins of water on Earth see chap. 1 in Harold V. Thurman and Alan P. Trujillo, *Essentials of Oceanography*, 7th ed. (Upper Saddle River, NJ: Prentice Hall, 2002).

Water Birth

All living beings on Earth are born of water. The earliest forms of life on Earth emerged through chemical processes in drops of water embraced by delicate membranes within the vast ocean womb.[10] These first single-celled beings thrived and filled the early ocean. As these beings evolved and complexified, water enabled multicellular life forms to emerge. When these reproduced they released their gametes (sperm and eggs) into the waters, where they joined to form new life. The earliest plants and animals to leave the oceans still required water to reproduce. Mosses and ferns relied on wet soil as a medium for spores to swim toward eggs. Amphibians returned to water to lay eggs and to fertilize them. Later plants, such as conifers, developed internal ponds in their cones that trapped windblown spores. Lizards acquired leathery eggshells that kept the watery environment within the egg secure on arid land. Flowering plants produced liquid nectar to attract pollinators as well as to provide moist channels that drew sperm toward eggs. Mammals and other animals with live birth developed internal, ocean wombs where new life was nourished.

As plants and animals covered the continents their exhalation released water vapor into the air. As water filled them and passed through their bodies, living beings became part of the hydrological cycle on which they depended for life. Water evaporated from oceans and blew across continents, where it returned to Earth as rain. The water pooled, puddled, and returned to the ocean through streams after refreshing, sustaining, and cleansing both land and living beings. The cycles of wet and dry changed and fluctuated throughout the history of Earth. Initial periods of sustained hydrological regularity allowed life to flourish and take root. New expressions of life later emerged from the land because of the constancy as well as the fluctuations of the hydrological cycle.

Water in Our Own Bodies

Without an abundance of water, humans would not exist.[11] Water is essential in mammalian biology. Like most mammals, humans are approximately 70 percent water. While water may be most evident in our tears,

10. For more on the origins of life on Earth see chap. 5 in Swimme and Berry, *The Universe Story*; Ward and Brownlee, *Rare Earth*; and chaps. 5 and 6 in Delsemme, *Our Cosmic Origins*.

11. For more on water's essential role in our bodies see chap. 8 in Jean P. Milani, Biological Sciences Curriculum Study, et al., *Biological Science: A Molecular Approach* 6th ed. (Lexington, MA.: D. C. Heath, 1990).

sweat, and urine, water permeates every system in our bodies, saturates every cell, and moistens every breath. Although a complete and detailed account of all the ways in which water makes an individual life possible is beyond the scope of this work, a strong sense of water's presence and participation in our own bodies is essential to our appreciation of water. To develop this personal appreciation, we consider the story of water at the cellular level. Examining water from a cellular perspective allows for the discussion of many of our vital systems and allows us to recognize water's constant presence throughout our bodies.

A human body is composed of trillions of cells. These cells contain organelles with functions similar to the body's organs. Each cell breathes, eats, and senses its environment. To be healthy, a person has to be healthy all the way down to the cellular level. Water is the medium that maintains health at this most basic level.

The watery drop that fills the membrane of the cell is called cytoplasm. Within it are organelles that carry out the cell's metabolic functions, such as mitochondria, which derive energy from oxygen, and ribosomes, which assemble proteins. Within the buoyancy of the cytoplasm, molecules and minerals needed by the organelles are diffused and distributed. Water's extraordinary capacity as a solvent allows the cytoplasm to hold the necessary ingredients in suspension until they are needed by the cell. This same capacity to dissolve allows water to absorb the wastes created by the cell and diffuse them out of its membrane.

The cytoplasm, which maintains communication between the organelles within the cell, is also in contact with the watery environment outside the cell through the cell's membrane. At least one side of every living cell is continually bathed in intercellular fluids. These fluids are enriched through our body's circulatory system. Blood that has been in contact with our digestive tract and lungs carries nutrients and oxygen to the cells. The blood, made mostly of water, dissolves the particles and carries them to every cell in the body. At the end of tiny capillaries, nutrients cross the blood vessel membranes and diffuse into the intercellular fluid that bathes the cells. The particles diffuse across the cell membrane and flood into the cell as they are needed. Waste from the cell crosses the membrane into the intercellular fluid, where it is absorbed and carried away. The blood brings this waste to the lungs, where it is released in exhalation, or to the kidneys, where it is released in urine. This contact between cellular and intercellular fluid allows the cell, as well as the body, to thrive and continue its functions of metabolism, reproduction, and repair.

The processes at the cellular level are recapitulated and completed by our whole body. Our lungs collect the oxygen needed by the cells and our breath releases their exhalation. Our digestive tract provides the nutrients for the cells' digestion and removes their waste. The water we drink floats and fills the cells that provide life to every part of our bodies. When we look at our hands we can imagine our life in miniature living in every living cell. When we look beyond ourselves we can see the same life forces flowing in every living being: plant, animal, and human. We know water provides life not only to ourselves but also to every cell of each being that lives, has lived, and will continually do so in each being born on Earth.

Water's story, like the stories of all things, began 13.7 billion years ago with hydrogen, but only after hundreds of millions of years did water itself emerge. With it new possibilities of creativity flowed into the Universe. As water assists in the birth of stars and accompanies the formation of planets, it also helped to form the Earth. Water cooled Earth, wrapping it in a fluid blanket that allowed Earth's creativity to flourish. All life on Earth—from the very first single-celled beings in the oceans, to the plants and animals that cover the continents, to ourselves—begins in bodies of water the size of oceans, eggs, or wombs. Water bathes every cell of each living being and maintains each life by ferrying nutrients and energy within the cell as well as between the cells of the entire organism. All beings are constantly washed by water that sustains the life and creativity of Earth. The implications of water's creative and sustaining presence to sacramentality are discussed in the final section of this chapter.

THE SACRAMENTAL STORY OF WATER

The creative and sustaining presence of water we see in the scientific story recurs in the sacramental story of water. This story traces water's role within the sacramental lineage of the Catholic tradition. The story begins at the headwaters of Christian sacramentality, the Old Testament. Since the Bible flows with narratives about water, only the most prominent passages of the Old Testament that are traditionally related to baptism are included here. Similarly, our discussion of water in the New Testament is limited to narratives with a baptismal character. After surveying biblical sources of water in baptism, the sacramental story of water turns to consider baptism in the early Christian church. As a means to filter through the extant materials, patristic blessings of water and instructions to candidates for baptism serve as the source of this part of water's story. From the early lessons of the church the sacramental story continues with the contemporary use of water in the Easter Vigil and current instructions to baptismal candidates.

Water's Biblical Source

> Blessed are you, Ever-Present God,
>   Creator of the Universe,
>   Through you we have the gift of water for baptism.
> This water of Stars, Earth, and Life you give
>   to bring us into fullness of life in you.
> This is the water over which your Spirit hovered at the Beginning,
>   the water that cleansed the Earth in Noah's day,
>   through which the Israelites passed unharmed
>   in Moses' day,
>   and in which Jesus was baptized.
> This is the water Jesus calmed,
>   the water he turned into wine in Cana,
>   and that flowed from his side on Calvary.

Old Testament

The biblical traditions recognize two kinds of water: flowing, living water and stale water that collects in cisterns.[12] While collected water is only fit for ordinary household purposes, living water participates in a greater mystery. Living water feeds streams, wells, and the sea. It rains from the vault of heaven and swells up from the depths. This living water is the source and sustenance of life as well as the flood that destroys it, the miraculous water that renders fields fertile and restores faith. It cleanses physically as well as spiritually. This water fills the well that never runs

12. For a complete discussion of the ancient and biblical understandings of water see Gerhard Kittel, Geoffrey W. Bromiley, and Gerhard Friedrich, eds., *Theological Dictionary of the New Testament*, 10 vols. (Grand Rapids: Eerdmans, 1964), 6:595–607; 8:314–33.

dry. The following four stories—Creation, The Great Flood, Exodus, and Crossing the Jordan—show God's reflection in living water.

Creation

The Bible begins with a story of creation in which God is alone with darkness and watery chaos. In each of the six days of creation God orders the world and brings forth creation through commands, then calls the creation good.

> In the beginning when God created the heavens and the earth, the earth was a formless void and darkness covered the face of the deep, while a wind from God swept over the face of the waters. Then God said, "Let there be light"; and there was light. And God saw that the light was good; and God separated the light from the darkness. God called the light Day, and the darkness he called Night. And there was evening and there was morning, the first day.
>
> And God said, "Let there be a dome in the midst of the waters, and let it separate the waters from the waters." So God made the dome and separated the waters that were under the dome from the waters that were above the dome. And it was so. God called the dome Sky. And there was evening and there was morning, the second day.
>
> And God said, "Let the waters under the sky be gathered together into one place, and let the dry land appear." And it was so. God called the dry land Earth, and the waters that were gathered together he called Seas. And God saw that it was good. . . .
>
> And God said, "Let the waters bring forth swarms of living creatures, and let birds fly above the Earth across the dome of the sky." So God created the great sea monsters and every living creature that moves, of every kind, with which the waters swarm, and every winged bird of every kind. And God saw that it was good. (Genesis 1:1-10, 20-21)

God does not work alone, but creates the world through the medium of water.[13] In the first story of the Bible, God's Spirit moves across the face of the waters before creation begins. Present with the water, God creates light and then day and night. Creation continues with God

---

13. As noted by Catherine Keller, until the beginning of the third century Jewish and Christian theologians did not have the notion of creation *ex nihilo* but rather took for granted that God created the world from unformed matter. For a complete treatment of the idea of creation from chaos and the controversial implications of its suppression see Catherine Keller, *Face of the Deep: A Theology of Becoming* (New York: Routledge, 2005).

separating the waters with the dome of the sky and then gathering the waters below to expose dry land. The arrangement of water in the first three days stabilizes the world and provides the setting for subsequent creation. Once dry land is exposed "God said, 'Let the earth put forth vegetation . . .' And it was so." (Gen 1:11). Then God tells the waters to bring forth swarms of creatures. In both cases God commands creation and the land and the sea to bring forth life. God calls life into being and water produces it. There is a liturgical flow to these verses. The creation of the world in the first story of the Bible is a prayer of call and response presided over by God and joined by water.

The Great Flood

By the time of our second story generations have passed since the creation of the world and God has reason to lament. The people have fallen into sin and debauchery, with the exception Noah and his small family. God arranges for Noah to protect his family and two of each of the animals, wild and tame, while all other beings on Earth perish in a flood of wrath.

> . . . on that day all the fountains of the great deep burst forth, and the windows of the heavens were opened. The rain fell on the earth forty days and forty nights. . . .
>
> The flood continued forty days on the earth; and the waters increased, and bore up the ark, and it rose high above the earth. The waters swelled and increased greatly on the earth; and the ark floated on the face of the waters. The waters swelled so mightily on the earth that all the high mountains under the whole heaven were covered; the waters swelled above the mountains, covering them fifteen cubits deep. And all flesh died that moved on the earth, birds, domestic animals, wild animals, all swarming creatures that swarm on the earth, and all human beings; everything on dry land in whose nostrils was the breath of life died. He blotted out every living thing that was on the face of the ground, human beings and animals and creeping things and birds of the air; they were blotted out from the earth. Only Noah was left, and those that were with him in the ark. And the waters swelled on the earth for one hundred fifty days.
>
> But God remembered Noah and all the wild animals and all the domestic animals that were with him in the ark. And God made a wind blow over the earth, and the waters subsided; the fountains of the deep and the windows of the heavens were closed, the rain the from heavens was restrained, and the waters gradually receded from the earth. (Genesis 7:11b-12, 17-24, 8:1-5)

In this familiar story water carries God's intention. Water first floods the world with God's wrath and then subsides as God remembers Noah and those with him in the ark. Once again God's Spirit moves across the waters, dry land emerges, and the world is recreated. With creation restored, God promises never to flood the Earth again. The sign of God's pledge is a rainbow, which is formed by the interaction of water and light. God says: "When I bring clouds over the earth and the bow is seen in the clouds, I will see it and remember my covenant that is between me and you and every living creature of all flesh; and the waters shall never again become a flood to destroy all flesh" (Gen 9:14-15). On God's behalf water flows with anger, ebbs with mercy, and restrains destruction with prismatic splendor.

The Exodus

By the time of the Exodus, our third story, many more generations have passed and God's favor continues to rest on the Hebrew people. They are nomads who in the course of time become slaves in the land of Egypt. The story of Exodus is the story of the Hebrews' flight from slavery, their passage into the desert and into a new covenant with God.

> Then Moses stretched out his hand over the sea. The LORD drove the sea back by a strong east wind all night, and turned the sea into dry land; and the waters were divided. The Israelites went into the sea on dry ground, the waters forming a wall for them on their right and on their left. The Egyptians pursued, and went into the sea after them, all of Pharaoh's horses, chariots, and chariot drivers. At the morning watch the LORD in the pillar of fire and cloud looked down upon the Egyptian army, and threw the Egyptian army into panic. He clogged their chariot wheels so that they turned with difficulty. The Egyptians said, "Let us flee from the Israelites, for the LORD is fighting for them against Egypt."
>
> Then the LORD said to Moses, "Stretch out your hand over the sea, so that the water may come back upon the Egyptians, upon their chariots and chariot drivers." So Moses stretched out his hand over the sea, and at dawn the sea returned to its normal depth. As the Egyptians fled before it, the LORD tossed the Egyptians into the sea. The waters returned and covered the chariots and the chariot drivers, the entire army of Pharaoh that had followed them into the sea; not one of them remained. But the Israelites walked on dry ground through the sea, the waters forming a wall for them on their right and on their left. (Exodus 14:21-29)

In this story of the Israelites' escape from slavery and their subsequent formation as a nation, water actualizes God's intention. Once again a wind blows over the water, restraining it to expose dry land. The Israelites pass between the walls of water to freedom while the Egyptian army is destroyed beneath the water's depths. As in the story of the flood, those judged worthy are saved while the forces of oppression are eliminated by water and God's will. The Israelites enter a new relationship with God when they cross the sea. They wander the desert, relying on God for direction, protection, and water. God's compassion for Israel is manifest in the cloud they follow by day and the oases they find on the way to the Promised Land.

Crossing the Jordan

The Israelites' time in the desert begins and ends with remarkable water crossings. In the Crossing of the Jordan, our fourth story, after forty years of wandering, the Israelites finally reach the banks of the Jordan River. All but Moses are allowed to cross into the Promised Land.

> On that very day the LORD addressed Moses as follows: "Ascend this mountain . . . and view the land of Canaan, which I am giving to the Israelites for a possession; you shall die there on the mountain that you ascend and shall be gathered to your kin, as your brother Aaron died on Mount Hor and was gathered to his kin; because both of you broke faith with me among the Israelites at the waters of Meribath-kadesh in the wilderness of Zin, by failing to maintain my holiness among the Israelites. Although you may view the land from a distance, you shall not enter it—the land that I am giving to the Israelites." (Deuteronomy 32:48-52)

> When the people set out from their tents to cross over the Jordan, the priests bearing the ark of the covenant were in front of the people. Now the Jordan overflows all its banks throughout the time of harvest. So when those who bore the ark had come to the Jordan, and the feet of the priests bearing the ark were dipped in the edge of the water, the waters flowing from above stood still, rising up in a single heap far off at Adam, the city that is beside Zarethan, while those flowing toward the sea of the Arabah, the Dead Sea, were wholly cut off. Then the people crossed over opposite Jericho. While all Israel were crossing over on dry ground, the priests who bore the ark of the covenant of the LORD stood on dry ground in the middle of the Jordan, until the entire nation finished crossing over the Jordan. (Joshua 3:14-17)

In this less familiar story of the crossing of the Jordan River, water once more reflects God's judgment and becomes the threshold of new life. When the Israelites cross the Jordan they end forty years of wandering in the desert. Although there have been many transgressions, God forgives them and allows the people to cross into the Promised Land. Moses alone is forbidden to cross the river because he broke faith with God at Meribath where, years before, instead of calling water from a stone Moses angrily struck the stone twice. It is not clear if Moses' sin is anger, disobedience, or lack of faith. Mishandling this one incident of bringing forth water brought down God's harsh judgment.

Having retained God's favor, the Israelites cross the Jordan dry-shod as they once crossed the Red Sea. At this crossing, however, there is no wind; instead, God's presence is carried over the water in the ark of the covenant. The ark that once kept Noah's flock dry is recalled in this story by the ark that the priests carry over the river, which causes the flow of the river to stop so that these chosen people can cross the river on dry ground. The Promised Land is entered and, in a land flowing with milk and honey, Israel's new life begins.

☩ ☩ ☩ ☩☩ ☩

In each of these Old Testament stories water carries God's intention. Water participates with God in creation and judgment and marks the threshold of new life. Water is central both to the initial creation of the world and to its destruction in the flood. When God remembers Noah and is moved to mercy, the waters subside. Subsequent rainbows remind God never to end all life on Earth with water. In the stories of Moses, water reveals God's judgment by serving as an agent of both delivery and destruction. Crossing water carries the assurance of God's presence and the beginning of a new phase of life. We now continue to explore water's reflections in the central stories of the New Testament.

New Testament

The New Testament brims with water. Jesus healed with water and preached from boats and lakeshores. He commanded a raging sea to silence and walked on its waves, inviting Peter to do the same. Jesus changed water into wine, he was baptized in water, and water flowed with blood from his side on Calvary. Throughout the gospels water reveals Jesus' divine power by mirroring Old Testament stories. Jesus' interactions with water evoke ancient stories of creation, judgment, and passage into new life. The following three stories—The Baptism of Jesus, The Wedding at Cana, and Calvary—have been selected to represent water in the New Testament because they are central to baptism, are at the heart of the Christian text, and show God's reflection in living water.

The Baptism of Jesus

Mark's gospel, perhaps the first to be written, begins with the baptism of Jesus in a succinctly worded passage that recalls the stories of the creation, the flood, and the crossing of the Jordan: "In those days Jesus came from Nazareth of Galilee and was baptized by John in the Jordan. And just as he was coming up out of the water, he saw the heavens torn apart and the Spirit descending like a dove on him. And a voice came from heaven, 'You are my Son, the Beloved; with you I am well pleased'" (Mark 1:9-11).

This baptismal account is full of intertextual echoes from previous stories. Jesus' baptism marks the beginning of a new era in history, and once again a creation story drenched in water is presented. It illustrates the Spirit of God upon the water and God's judgment regarding its goodness. It is in the Jordan River that Jesus is baptized, the same river through which God granted the Israelites passage into the Promised Land. The Spirit of God appearing as a dove recalls the dove that brought the promise of dry land and new life to Noah in the ark. The voice of God recalls the divine wind that blew across the waters at creation, dried the flood, and separated the Red Sea. With these biblical themes in play, Jesus' baptism is revealed as a new moment of creation, judgment, and passage into new life.

The Wedding at Cana

In this second story, the Wedding at Cana, Jesus, his mother, and his disciples attend a wedding in Cana, in Galilee, in the land the Hebrews entered when they crossed the Jordan. Here Jesus begins his ministry with the transformation of water.

> On the third day there was a wedding in Cana of Galilee, and the mother of Jesus was there. Jesus and his disciples had also been invited to the wedding. When the wine gave out, the mother of Jesus said to him, "They have no wine." And Jesus said to her, "Woman, what concern is that to you and to me? My hour has not yet come." His mother said to the servants, "Do whatever he tells you." Now standing there were six stone water jars for the Jewish rites of purification, each holding twenty or thirty gallons. Jesus said to them, "Fill the jars with water." And they filled them up to the brim. He said to them, "Now draw some out, and

take it to the chief steward." So they took it. When the steward tasted the water that had become wine, and did not know where it came from (though the servants who had drawn the water knew), the steward called the bridegroom and said to him, "Everyone serves the good wine first, and then the inferior wine after the guests have become drunk. But you have kept the good wine until now." Jesus did this, the first of his signs, in Cana of Galilee, and revealed his glory; and his disciples believed in him. (John 2:1-11)

The first miracle story in John's gospel involves water. As God does in Genesis, so also Jesus creates through water, and the steward calls the creation good. The water transformed into wine is drawn from stone jars brimming with living water for purification rites that recall water's role in cleansing and judgment from earlier stories. This miracle takes place in Cana, a name that recalls "Canaan," the Promised Land the Israelites entered as they crossed the Jordan. That Jesus' first miracle occurs at this location (and during a wedding celebration) signifies the beginning of a new phase of life. With an act of creation from water Jesus crosses a threshold into public ministry, his disciples believe in him, and a new relationship between God and the world begins.

Calvary
Our third story takes a darker turn. We come to the cross, where we contemplate the mystery of water in the most desolate of Christian stories. In this passage from the crucifixion narrative water is present even at Jesus' death: "But when they came to Jesus and saw that he was already dead, they did not break his legs. Instead, one of the soldiers pierced his side with a spear, and at once blood and water came out" (John 19:33-34).

Water is the key to a hope-filled reading of this horrific passage. The mixture of water and blood that flow from Jesus' side convinces the soldiers that Jesus is dead. However, even before the story continues, the mention of water hints at the possibility of new life. The presence of water anticipates a new creation: a threshold is crossed; God is present. At the beginning of Jesus' ministry water and wine herald the crossing of a threshold in the relationship between God and the world. Here on Calvary, as Earth receives the water and blood that flow from Jesus' side, we dare to hope for yet another passage into a deeper covenant with God. A new phase of life is coming. The tomb is not the final word, because the water that accompanies Jesus' death foreshadows his resurrection. In water there is present, even in this dreadful story, the hope that the tomb of death will become a womb of new life for Jesus and for his followers.

In this brief survey we have seen how water reflects God in passages of the Bible that relate directly to baptism. In the Old Testament, in the first creation account in Genesis, water exists with God before the beginning of creation. How water came to be, or if it always existed, is not revealed. The creation story simply begins with water. For the first days of creation God creates through the arrangement of water and then, with God, water produces all the creatures that fill the seas. The stories of Noah and Moses demonstrate that water moves with God's wrath and God's mercy. Water floods and destroys, relents and allows life to enter into newness. Water also reminds God to refrain from destruction. In the New Testament, water reveals Jesus' divinity through stories that echo Old Testament stories of God. Jesus' baptism is shown as a new moment of creation, as are the beginning of his ministry in Cana, and his death at Calvary.

More stories from both testaments could be told. There are stories of water found in the desert and of water offered to strangers and prophets. There are stories of floods, waves, and lakes, as well as stories of rest, healing, and yearnings fulfilled. There are stories of storms and seas subdued to silence and hymns in which hail and rain are called to sing praise. Each encounter with water reveals God's closeness and power, God's judgment, and God's creative and sustaining presence. Biblical stories of water are the fount from which the Christian baptismal tradition emerged.

WATER IN THE BAPTISMAL TRADITION

Blessed are you, Ever-Present God,
  Creator of the Universe,
  Through you we have the gift of water for baptism.
Your Spirit continuously moves within water.
  Enliven the water in this font and in us
  so we may remember that all water flows
  with your holy presence.

Now that we have navigated water's cosmic, earthly, and biblical tributaries we arrive at the baptismal tradition itself. From here we follow the flow of blessings and instructions to candidates for baptism from the second-century *Didache* to the seventh-century Gelasian Sacramentary, and end with the current teachings in the Rite of Christian Initiation for Adults.

Patristic Understandings of Water In Baptism

Baptism has always held a central place in the belief and praxis of Christians. This section of the sacramental story of water explores patristic teachings regarding the significance, both cosmic and personal, of Jesus' baptism. Water's story continues as we trace the sacramental history of baptism in the writings of early theologians.

The Significance of Water in Jesus' Baptism

Theologians of the early church believed that the world shifted when Jesus was baptized in the waters of the Jordan River. Jesus' baptism was a new moment of creation, a moment that restored sanctifying power to water and consecrated all creation with divine presence. No longer were humans exiled from the Garden: the Garden itself was restored and flowed with God's presence. Moreover, each person could enter into this new creation of restored relationship with the divine by passing through the waters of baptism.

In his study on the baptism of Jesus the distinguished Benedictine theologian Kilian McDonnell retrieves three patristic understandings of the cosmic significance of Jesus' baptism: universal baptism, new creation, and cosmic consecration.[14] In a passage recreated from fragments of a text written between 165 and 175, Melito of Sardis speaks of universal baptism, the baptism of heavenly bodies, and the rightness of "creation's captain" following suit:

> If you wish to observe the heavenly bodies being baptized, make haste now to the Ocean, and there I will show you a strange sight. If you look there you will see the heavenly bodies being baptized. At the end of the day they make haste to the Ocean, there to go down into the waters, into the outspread sea, and boundless main, and infinite deep, and immeasurable

---

14. For a thorough exploration of the cosmic significance of Jesus' baptism see Kilian McDonnell, *The Baptism of Jesus in the Jordan: The Trinitarian and Cosmic Order of Salvation* (Collegeville, MN: Liturgical Press, 1996).

Ocean, and pure water. The sun sinks into the sea, and when it has been bathed in symbolic baptism, it comes up exultantly from the waters, rising as a new sun, purified from the bath. What the sun does, so do the stars and moon. They bathe in the sun's swimming pool like good disciples. By this baptism, sun, moon, and stars are soaking up pure brilliance. . . . Should it be a matter of surprise that Christ, the king of heaven and creation's captain, a Sun out of heaven, should be bathed in the Jordan?[15]

For Melito baptism in water is an ongoing process in which all of creation naturally participates. In other passages Melito speaks of forged metals dipped in water, the Earth bathed in rain, land renewed by the Nile's flood, and air washed in raindrops. Jesus was baptized in water because everything is baptized in water. Jesus' baptism was part of the universal baptismal liturgy.

New creation is the second patristic understanding of the cosmic significance of water identified by McDonnell. Irenaeus of Lyons (d. 202) writes that God's Spirit, who once hovered over the waters of creation, was again present when the Holy Spirit hovered over the waters of the Virgin's womb at the moment of Jesus' conception. For Irenaeus baptismal water, beginning with that of the Jordan, was the womb of spiritual birth. Tertullian (ca. 160–225) writes, "[The Spirit] rests on the waters of baptism as if he recognized there his ancient throne, the one who under the form of a dove descended on the Savior."[16] Cyril of Jerusalem (ca. 315–386) notices that both Genesis and the gospels start with water, implying that no new age is possible without water. Finally, Gregory of Nazianzus (ca. 330–389) imagines Jesus carrying the cosmos out of the baptismal water with him. These church fathers teach that water accompanies new creation and that all creation is renewed by water.

Cosmic consecration is the third and final cosmic implication of water McDonnell finds in early church writings. Clement of Alexandria (ca. 150–215) teaches that the purpose of Jesus' baptism was to sanctify the waters. Later, Jacob of Serugh (ca. 451–521) emphatically says that when Jesus stepped into the Jordan, "the entire nature of the waters perceived that you had visited them—seas, deeps, rivers, springs, and pools all thronged together to receive the blessing from your footsteps."[17] This blessing was not limited to water. The early Armenian catechism, *The*

---

15. Quoted in ibid., 50–51.
16. Ibid., 54.
17. Ibid., 61.

Teaching of St. Gregory (ca. 490), teaches that creation itself was exiled from the Garden when Adam sinned. The curse of separation from God did not fall on humans alone. Thus the blessing of Jesus' footsteps in the Jordan rippled through all the waters of creation and into the entire created order. Through the water of Jesus' baptism all of creation is once again made sacred.

The significance of Jesus' baptism was not only cosmic, but also personal. Each believing Christian was born into the new creation initiated in Jesus' baptism by entering the womb and tomb of baptism. Justin Martyr (ca. 100–165) was the earliest writer to use the image of the womb for baptismal waters. He describes a baptismal ceremony in which the washing with water is followed by reading the verse of John's gospel: ". . . no one can see the kingdom of God without being born from above" (John 3:3). Two centuries later, Cyril of Jerusalem (ca. 315–386) compared the three pourings of water in baptism to the three days Christ spent in the tomb. He writes, "At one and the same time you were dying and being born, and that saving water became at once your grave and your mother."[18] A century later Pope Leo the Great, who reigned from 440 to 461, beautifully interwove the themes of baptismal waters and Mary's womb:

> The beginning that He took in the womb of the Virgin, He put into the fountain of baptism; He gave to the water what He gave to His mother; power of the Most High and the overshadowing of the Holy Spirit, which made Mary give birth to the Savior, the same caused the water to give a second birth to the believer. For every [person] reborn, the water of baptism is like the womb of the Virgin: the same Holy Spirit who filled the Virgin fills the fountain.[19]

In the womb and tomb waters of baptism a person dies to sin, is cleansed and recreated, and then is born into the new creation of the reign of God.

Since its inception the church has recognized both cosmic and personal significance in the baptism of Jesus. The concept of universal baptism celebrates that all creation is renewed through a continuous baptism in water—a baptism in which Jesus took part as "creation's captain." New creation is evident in the story of Jesus' baptism though the parallels to

18. Paul F. Palmer, ed., *Sacraments and Worship: Liturgy and Doctrinal Development of Baptism, Confirmation, and the Eucharist*, Sources of Christian Theology 1 (Westminster, MD: Newman Press, 1955), 13.

19. Ibid., 76–77.

more ancient creation stories and the presence of water. As Jesus enters the waters of the Jordan a cosmic consecration resounds through the world and restores God's blessing to all creation. Perhaps most significantly to Christian believers, each person is invited to enter this new creation and blessing through the waters of baptism.

Instructions and Blessings of Water

The sacramental story of water begins with the first creation narrative in Genesis. From there the story of water ripples outward through the Old Testament and then the New Testament, where water takes on its baptismal meaning. In ever widening circles the story of water spreads through the early church as theologians delve into the significance of Jesus' baptism. All sacramental stories of water have the creation account and the baptism of Jesus at their centers.

The continuation of water's story can be traced in transformations in the celebration of the baptismal liturgy. Fortunately, Paul Palmer has collected the extant sacramental instructions, blessings, and liturgies of the early church in his authoritative book, *Sacraments and Worship*.[20] Using this resource as a guide, we now trace the history of blessings and teachings about water in baptism. This history reflects the centrality of the scriptural themes of God's creative and sustaining presence in water while at the same time showing the gradual disappearance of living water in baptismal rituals.

The earliest references to baptism do not include a blessing for water. The author of the *Didache* (ca. 70–160) writes: "Baptize in running water. But if you have no running water, baptize in other water; and if you cannot in cold, then in warm. But if you have neither, pour water over the head three times."[21] *The Apostolic Tradition of Hippolytus* (ca. 215) instructs those who will be baptized to rise early and "pray over the water" so that when they came to it, the water would be "pure and flowing." Both of these sources stress the physical condition of the water and do not include a blessing for the water. For at least the first two hundred years of Christian tradition water was not blessed for baptism. Clean, living water did not need to be blessed.

At the end of the fourth century we find the first discussion of a blessing of water in Ambrose of Milan's writings, where he compares the water

20. Ibid.
21. Ibid., 1.

of baptism with the water of Marah. Three days after the Israelites crossed the Red Sea they were in the desert without water when they came to Marah. The water there was bitter and could not be drunk. Moses cried out to the Lord, who showed him a piece of wood. Moses threw the wood into the water and the water became sweet. The people drank and the Lord led them to a place to camp with twelve springs of water and seventy palm trees (Exod 15:22-27). Ambrose writes: "As then Moses, the Prophet, cast wood into that fountain, so also the priest casts the proclamation of the cross into this fountain and the water becomes sweet for grace."[22]

Beginning in the fifth century we find that God's blessing of water has been displaced by the priest's blessing. The need for water to be blessed was emphasized by Augustine of Hippo (ca. 354–430), in his *Treatise on the Gospel of John*. Augustine writes: "Take away the word and what is water but water? The word is joined to the element and the result is a sacrament, itself becoming, in a sense, a visible word as well."[23] Water, once seen as having its own spiritual power, by this point needed a word of blessing to become effective.

The Gelasian Sacramentary is the first document to detail the ceremonies and prayers of baptism. Although named for Pope Gelasius, who reigned from 492 to 496, the sacramentary was probably compiled in the late seventh or early eighth century for use in the Frankish kingdom. Beginning with the primordial waters of Genesis, through the flood and the deliverance from Egypt, to the baptism, miracles, and death of Jesus, the Sacramentary recalls feats of participation of water in divine purpose. In this blessing, which was prayed for twelve hundred years, we can notice the multiple images of water, the poetic tone, and the sway of humility and majesty.

> O God, by whose unseen power
>   the wondrous effect of thy sacrament is wrought,
>   and unworthy as we are to perform so great a rite,
>   do not withdraw the gifts of Thy favor,
>   but incline the ears of Thy goodness even to our prayers.
> O God, whose Spirit in the very first beginnings of the world
>   did brood over the waters,
>   giving the element of water, even in its origin,
>   the power to sanctify;

22. Ibid., 19.
23. Ibid., 87.

Who by water didst wash away the crimes of a guilty world,
    and by the outpouring of the flood didst signify regeneration,
    so that one and the same element might have the
            mysterious power
    to make an end of vice and a beginning of virtue;
Look down, O Lord, upon the face of Thy Church
    and multiply within her Thy acts of regeneration,
    thou who makest the city glad by the flowing torrent of
        Thy grace
    and openest to the whole world the font of baptism
    for the renewal of the nations,
    so that under Thy great dominion
    they may receive from the Holy Spirit the grace of
    Thy only-begotten Son.
May this water, prepared for the rebirth of men,
    be rendered fruitful by the secret inpouring of His divine power;
    may a heavenly offspring, conceived in holiness and reborn
    into a new creation, come forth from the stainless womb
    of this divine font;
    and may all, however distinguished by age in time or sex
        in body,
    be brought into one new infancy by the motherhood of grace.
Begone then every unclean spirit at Thy bidding, Lord;
    begone all wicked and satanic wiles.
Let no power of opposition intrude here,
    spread its snares about this place,
    or creep into it by stealth,
    or taint it by poison.
May this holy and innocent creature be free from all the
        enemy's assaults
    and cleansed by the removal of all wickedness.
Be this fount of life, a water of new birth, a purifying stream,
    so that all who are to be washed in this bath of salvation may,
    by the working of the Holy Spirit within them,
    obtain the grace of perfect cleansing.
Therefore, I bless thee, water, God's creature,
    by the living God, by the true God, by the holy God;
    by that God whose word in the beginning
    separated thee from the dry land,
    and whose Spirit brooded over thee.

Who caused thee to flow from a well in paradise
    and bade thee water the whole earth in four streams.
Who, when thou wast bitter in the wilderness,
    poured sweetness into thee, making thee fit to drink,
    and brought thee out of a rock to quench His people's thirst.
I bless thee too through Jesus Christ, His only Son, our Lord,
    who in Cana of Galilee, by a wondrous miracle,
    changed thee into wine;
    whose feet walked upon thee,
    and who was baptized in thee by John in Jordan;
    who made thee flow out of His side, together with His blood,
    and commanded His disciples that believers should be
    baptized in thee,
    saying: Go teach all nations,
    baptizing them in the name of the Father
    and of the Son
    and of the Holy Ghost.
Almighty God, in Thy mercy stand by us who are
    observing this commandment.
Let thy gracious breath be upon us.
    With Thy own lips, bless this pure water,
    so that besides its natural power of cleansing bodies,
    it may have the effect of purifying souls.
May the power of the Holy Ghost descend into this brimming font.
    And may it make the whole substance of this water
    fruitful in regenerative power.
Here may all stain of sin be wiped away.
    Here let human nature, created in Thy likeness,
    and recreated to the honor of its maker,
    be cleansed of all ancestral defilement,
    so that every man who enters into
    this sacrament of regeneration
    may be born again into a new childhood of true innocence.
Through our Lord Jesus Christ, Thy Son:
    who will come to judge the living and the dead,
    and the world by fire.[24]

24. Ibid., 35–37.

It should be noted that the blessings of water became longer as the amounts of water used in baptism became smaller. Initially people were baptized outdoors in running rivers that were not blessed liturgically. As the Christian population grew and rituals were institutionalized, worship was moved into churches. Why were blessings instituted? One reason may be that instead of flowing rivers, indoor cisterns and then small fonts were used for baptism. Water in cisterns was not as fresh and perhaps as clean as flowing water. *Living water* had been replaced by stale *collected water*, fit for only household use. As Christianity became urbanized, the power and importance of water was no longer evident to all who participated in the baptismal liturgies, and consequently the church began to bless water.

The extended blessing in the sacramentary tells of water's role in salvation history and serves to remind people of their intimacy with water. The redundancy of the prayer reflects an oral tradition in which the stories of water were taught to people who did not read. The Gelasian Sacramentary was written in Latin, the common language of the people for whom the sacramentary was prepared. However, as the church spread and Latin gradually fell into disuse except as a scholarly language, the prayers that served to remind people of the stories now served to distance them even further. People at a baptismal liturgy could no longer understand the stories of water, only that a lengthy prayer was required to make the stale, nonliving water fit for baptism.

The prayers of the Gelasian Sacramentary, including this blessing of water, were used with only minor changes for twelve hundred years, from the eighth century until the liturgical reforms following Vatican II in the late twentieth century.[25] As we shall see from a comparison of the Gelasian blessing with the blessing in the current sacramentary, the significance of water has not been the focus of conversation since the Gelasian Sacramentary was compiled. The two blessings are remarkably similar. Even though much scholastic conversation concerned the metaphysics of matter—how substance and spirit interacted—the particulars of how an individual sacramental functioned were no longer debated. The similarity of the blessings reflects the absence of further development of these ideas. For that reason we continue the sacramental story of water with the current blessing of water used for baptism at the Easter Vigil

---

25. For a side-by-side comparison of the baptismal liturgy in the Gelasian Sacramentary and the 1888 Roman Pontifical see ibid., 25–37.

and the instructions to candidates for baptism from the Rite of Christian Initiation for Adults.

Contemporary Understanding of Water in Baptism

Water is prominent in the Easter Vigil. In well-celebrated liturgies water is ceremoniously and joyfully restored to dry baptismal fonts. Water's part in salvation history is told in the blessing and its role is once again enacted in baptism. The following prayer is the blessing of water used during the Easter Vigil. We can notice the differences, particularly the economy of expression, between this blessing and the Gelasian blessing quoted above.

Father,
you give us grace through sacramental signs,
which tell us of the wonders of your unseen power.

In baptism, we use your gift of water,
which you have made a rich symbol of the grace
you give us in this sacrament.

At the very dawn of creation
your Spirit breathed on the waters,
making them the wellspring of all holiness.

The waters of the great flood
you made a sign of the waters of baptism
that make an end to sin
and a new beginning of goodness.

Through the waters of the Red Sea
you led Israel out of slavery
to be an image of God's holy people,
set free from sin by baptism.

In the waters of the Jordan
your Son was baptized by John
and anointed with the Spirit.

Your Son willed that water and blood should flow from his side
as he hung upon the cross.

After his resurrection, he told his disciples:
"Go out and teach all nations,
baptizing them in the name of the Father, and of the Son,
and of the Holy Spirit."

Father,
look now with love upon your Church
and unseal for it the fountain of baptism.

By the power of the Holy Spirit
give to this water the grace of your Son,
so that in the sacrament of baptism
all those whom you have created in your likeness
may be cleansed from sin
and rise to a new birth of innocence
by water and the Holy Spirit.

We ask you, Father, with your Son
to send the Holy Spirit upon the waters of this font.
May all who are buried with Christ in the death of baptism
rise also with him to newness of life. (222)[26]

The first thing to be noticed about this blessing is that it is written in English for English-speaking people. Replacing the Latin of the Gelasian blessing with the vernacular greatly assists people attending an Easter Vigil to reconnect with the story of water. However, the next thing we notice about this blessing is its brevity. Many of the references in the ancient blessing to water's grace-filled moments are omitted in this modern prayer; it has no mention of rivers watering paradise, water flowing from rock in the desert, the miracle at Cana, or Jesus walking on water. In the shorter prayer the poetic tone is lost. Despite the best of intentions, this post–Vatican II text evacuates the rhythm and majesty of the previous text. This blessing does not evoke "flowing torrents of God's grace" nor does it ask God to bless the water with holy lips. Perhaps most significantly to this survey, even though our knowledge about water has

---

26. *The Rites of the Catholic Church*, vol. 1 (Collegeville, MN: Liturgical Press, 1990).

increased in the twelve hundred years since the writing of the Gelasian blessing, no new insights about water seeped into the new prayer.

In the *Catechism of the Catholic Church* (CCC),[27] the official magisterial teaching of the Catholic Church, the blessing of water is not about the water itself. Rather, the *Catechism* explains the blessing of water used during the Easter Vigil as a chronicle of the events in salvation history that prefigure baptism.

> The Church has seen in Noah's ark a prefiguring of salvation by Baptism, for by it "a few, that is eight persons, were saved through water" [1 Pet 3:20]. (1217)

> Since the beginning of the world, water, so humble and wonderful a creature, has been a source of life and fruitfulness. Sacred Scripture sees it as "overshadowed" by the Spirit of God. (1218)

> If water springing up from the earth symbolizes life, the water of the sea is a symbol of death and so can represent the mystery of the cross. By this symbolism Baptism signifies communion with Christ's death. (1220)

> Finally, Baptism is prefigured in the crossing of the Jordan River by which the People of God received the gift of the land promised to Abraham's descendants, an image of eternal life. (1222)

These few statements about water describe it as a humble participant in salvation history. Water is "overshadowed" by God and brings "life and fullness" as well as death. The comments on the significance of water in the Hebrew stories of creation, the great flood, and the crossing of the Jordan are restricted to the symbolic images that prefigure Christian baptism and add nothing more about water's cosmic journey or meaning. Although the biblical themes of creation, judgment, and passage into new life are retained along with the patristic insight of the waters of baptism as womb and tomb, the cosmic significance of Jesus' baptism is lost. There is no mention in the current blessing of the universality of baptism, of the cosmic consecration of all beings, or of Jesus' baptism as a new moment

---

27. *Catechism of the Catholic Church: Revised in Accordance with the Official Latin Text Promulgated by Pope John Paul II*, 2d ed. (Washington, DC: United States Catholic Conference, 1997).

of creation. In this prayer, water serves as only a "symbol of grace," no longer fecund with grace in its own right.

Beyond the narrative blessing of water in the liturgy, those participating in the baptism are told little about the water used. The study edition of the Rite of Christian Initiation for Adults (RCIA) says that the blessing of water "declares the religious meaning of water as God's creation and the sacramental use of water in the unfolding of the paschal mystery, and the blessing is also a remembrance of God's wonderful works in the history of salvation" (210).

Further instruction states that the washing that occurs in baptism "is not a mere purification rite but the sacrament of being joined to Christ" (213). These two statements are all that is said about water; there is no mandate in the RCIA to teach anything further. It is up to the particular team preparing candidates for baptism to determine whether or not any investigation of water's biblical, historical, or physical characteristics are explored. Although many RCIA instructors do an admirable job of instruction, what a person learns about water is based on the interests of her instructor.

Through this exploration of water in the Roman Catholic tradition as reflected in Scripture, blessings, and instructions to baptismal candidates we have moved in stages from a vital, immediate knowledge of water to a diluted symbolism. The earliest instructions were simple: use cold, flowing, living water. No blessing was required. As Christianity spread and was successful in cities, large churches were built and the faithful were no longer brought to flowing, living water for baptism. As living water was replaced with the stale water of cisterns, prayers of exorcism and blessing were used to purify the water and teach its stories. By the end of the seventh century, with the extensive blessing of water in the Gelasian Sacramentary, pedestal baptismal fonts had come into use. As the amount of water used in baptism lessened, the words of blessing swelled. Furthermore, as the common understanding of Latin diminished, the efficacy of the Gelasian blessing to recall the significance of water was lost. With a return to prayers in the vernacular, the English translation of the Sacramentary calls water a "symbol of grace." Water is now a metaphor for what it was once known to be in itself. It points to itself as a vessel drained of its symbolic fullness. In short, the sacramental significance of water shifted from a force of life and death that needed no explanation to a "humble creature" in need of blessing that merits no explanation.

COSMOCENTRIC SACRAMENTALITY AND WATER

We have explored 13.7 billion years of the stories of water. We traced water's epic voyage from the Beginning, when only primary particles and energy existed, through the emergence of water in stellar remnants, through the first life on Earth, and finally to the water in the cells of our own bodies. We have watched the ripples of water's sacramental story spread outward from the story of creation, through the stories of Noah and Moses, to stories of Jesus, and then to the blessings and teachings of the church. In its natural history the sense of water as a creating, sustaining presence deepens, while in the sacramental story awareness of water's presence diminishes. Integrating these two sets of stories has the potential to reawaken baptismal participants to the magnificence of God reflected in water. Moreover, the integration of the stories of water becomes the foundation for a cosmocentric sacramentality.

The concept of thresholds in the development of Earth described by Pierre Teilhard de Chardin in *The Human Phenomenon* is helpful in integrating the natural history and sacramental stories of water. [28] Teilhard noticed that on a round planet beings and energy tend to spread until they cover the planet, whereupon they fold back on themselves. He sees this folding over as one of the forces responsible for leaps—or thresholds—in the development of the Earth. Teilhard divides the story of Earth's development into four phases: pre-life, life, thought, and superlife. Water's story can be integrated using this same scheme.

The pre-life phase of water is the story of water's stellar birth and its role in the formation of stars and planets, including Earth. This phase continues as water fills the nascent oceans and bathes the continents with rain and streams. Water crosses the threshold into the life phase when life emerges on Earth. In this phase water surrounds, fills, and sustains the first life on Earth and every life since. This phase continues with stories of water in living bodies, including mammals such as us. Teilhard sets the

28. Pierre Teilhard de Chardin, *The Human Phenomenon*, trans. Sarah Appleton-Weber (Portland, OR: Sussex Academic Press, 2003).

threshold between the phases of life and thought at self-reflective consciousness. With the emergence of self-reflective consciousness in humans, water becomes conscious of itself. In this phase the focus shifts to what we humans think about water and the stories we tell about water. The phase of superlife in water emerges as human consciousness covers the planet and folds back upon itself. This folding brings the global reality of water into our consciousness. In this phase ecological imbalances caused by human indifference are no longer ignored. Issues of water pollution, scarcity, and global health become invitations to enter into Earth-centered relationships in which we begin to realize that we are not separate from water or from any other part of the Earth community. We are, in fact, composed of water more than of anything else. The activity of water within and around us makes our living, even our thoughts, possible. We are *Aqua sapiens*: water thinking, water aware of itself. As *Aqua sapiens* we know that the water of our bodies is part of the hydrological cycle that animates Earth.

In summary, through these developmental stages the emphasis in the story of water shifts from the inorganic, to the living, to human thought, and finally to water's cosmic nature. In this final stage we experience ourselves not only in our particular human lineage but also in our aqueous lineage, which stretches back 13.7 billion years to the Beginning and reaches ahead into the future. Teilhard's concept of thresholds in Earth's development places the aware person within the swirling natural history and sacramental story of water.

What might this awareness of oneself as absorbed in water's story mean to a person about to be baptized? Within this cosmocentric perspective at least four insights emerge. First, she realizes that the natural history of water deepens the wisdom conveyed in the sacramental tradition. She sees salvation history beginning in the cosmic history of water. This history does not contradict the religious story, but provides further evidence of the wisdom of early theologians. For example, she notices that in both the scientific story of creation and in Genesis, water preexisted the creation of Earth. She feels the resonances between the natural history as it tells of oceans covering the young Earth until dry land emerged and the Genesis story as it tells of water blown aside until dry land appeared. She also knows that water participates in births, from stars to primal life to her own, and sees in that the wisdom of marking her spiritual rebirth in water as well.

A second insight of a person immersed within the story of water might be that water has participated in sacramentality since it first existed in the Universe. She learns that a sacrament is a blessing from God and a response from a created being. As a water being she feels the cosmic and sacramental stories of water pulsing in her veins. The beat of her heart reminds her of water's responsiveness to God's blessing of creation through its assistance in birth and its sustenance of life. Moreover, she experiences water as a medium through which God is revealed. Out of water's proclivity to respond to and mediate God's blessings, creation continues, life on Earth flourishes, and she comes to a deeper knowledge of God.

A third insight concerns the nature of blessing. A cosmically-minded person approaching baptism is sure that water has flowed with God's blessing ever since it emerged billions of years ago. The *Catechism of the Catholic Church* teaches that the action of the first person of the Trinity, God the Creator, is to bless. God continually blesses (1078–1079). During her baptismal studies she learns that God blesses the world as it is created. She learns also that the blessing is restored to creation after the flood, and again when Jesus enters the waters of his baptism. Through both the natural history and the sacramental stories she knows that blessings accompany water. In both cases water sustains life. It is clear to her that God's blessing indwells all water. Therefore she senses that the blessing most appropriate for water at baptism is one that acknowledges that God's primal blessing has always permeated water. Such a blessing should proclaim the 13.7-billion-year history of water's role in salvation history and begin to restore the sacred relationship between water and the human participants in baptism.

A fourth insight of the baptismal candidate is the recognition of the underlying unity all living beings share because of water. She delights that she takes part in a universal baptism—a baptism that washes everything on the face of the Earth and in the oceans. She recalls that early theologians taught that the Sun, Moon, and stars all dipped into baptismal waters each night to rise cleansed in the morning. She marvels at Melito's intuition about water's historic relationship to these celestial beings. She knows that the water in which she will be baptized helped birth Earth and the Solar System. She remembers that God's sustaining presence is essential to her continuing existence and, at least in part, this continual presence is achieved through the intricate interactions of water within the cells of her body. She knows that Earth flows with God's presence in rainwater, in ocean water, and in the blood of her own veins. As she looks at her hand she realizes that it exists because of the gift of water. More than this, as she looks across the human congregation gathered to celebrate her baptism and then beyond to the plants and animals that surround the church she knows that all living beings participate with her in these same blessings through water.

A Blessing of Water

Blessed are you, Ever-Present God,
    Creator of the Universe,
    Through you we have the gift of water for baptism.

Water that formed in the remnants of ancient stars
    and brought our Day Star to birth.
Water that cooled the nascent Earth.
    Rising from deep within and carried by comets,
    your water drenched our young planet
    and covered it in oceans
Water that birthed the first life on Earth
    and each life thereafter
Water that fills and flows within every living being.

This water of Stars, Earth, and Life you give
    to bring us into fullness of life in you.
This is the water over which your Spirit hovered at the Beginning,
    the water that cleansed the Earth in Noah's day,
    through which the Israelites passed unharmed
    in Moses' day,
    and in which Jesus was baptized.
This is the water that Jesus calmed,
    the water he turned into wine in Cana,
    and that flowed from his side on Calvary.

Ever-Present God, your Spirit continuously moves within water.
    Enliven the water in this font and in us
    so we may remember that all water flows
    with your holy presence.

Blessed are you, Ever-Present God,
    Creator of the Universe,
    Through you we have the gift of water for baptism.

Chapter Two

OIL

In Praise of Oil

> Loving and Living God, we rejoice
>   in your gift of Olive Oil for baptism,
>
> Oil that cradled nascent life in ancient oceans,
> Oil that embraces every cell of every being that ever lived,
> Oil that stores the generosity of the Sun,
> Oil that glistened on Aaron's face and beard,
>   and whose miraculous abundance
>   we celebrate at Chanukah.
> Oil of widows and bridesmaids, radiant with fidelity,
> Oil of anointing, presence of God made visible,
>   hovering over the waters of creation,
>   bearing the olive branch to Noah after the flood,
>   appearing above the Jordan to announce
>   Jesus as your beloved.
> Oil of baptism that heals and seals us in your love.
>
> Loving and living God, we rejoice
>   in your gift of Olive Oil for baptism.

The story of oil is a story of generosity and joy. It is a story of a life-giving embrace, of the caress that touches all living beings. Every living cell

37

forms within an oily wrap and is forever cradled by it. This thin coating is the membrane that holds the living cell together and allows it to communicate with other cells. Without oil the cell could not survive. Without oil to form a membrane, life as we know it would not exist on Earth. Oil nurtures life. It collects in drops within plant cells where it is stored as nutrients for the plant as well as for the animals that consume it. Olive oil is particularly generous to human communities. In Mediterranean cultures olives were perhaps the first trees cultivated. Since ancient days the abundant yield of olive trees has provided fruit as well as oil for almost every domestic need. Olive oil is not used for harsh purposes. In its domestic use it provides lighting and healing, comfort and care. In its ritual use it signifies dedication to God as well as God's blessing and presence.

The prayer that begins this chapter is a blessing of oil inspired by my reflections on the scientific and sacred stories of oil. Unlike water, my meditations with olive oil elicited a brief, celebratory hymn rather than a ballad that revealed oil's full story. As we see in the following pages, it is the nature of olive oil to be both modest and joyful.

THE NATURAL HISTORY OF OLIVE OIL

As with all things, the story of olive oil begins with the birth of the Universe when the first drops of matter formed. All the elements found in olive oil—its nitrogen, oxygen, sodium, calcium, and iron—emerged in stars of every different size. Eventually these elements mixed in space with many others and found their way to the third ring around the Sun, which formed the planet Earth.[1] The story of olive oil continues in the oceans of Earth.

Oceans to Olives

> *Loving and Living God, we rejoice*
> *in your gift of Olive Oil for baptism,*
> *Oil that cradled nascent life in ancient oceans,*
> *Oil that embraces every cell of every being that ever lived,*
> *Oil that stores the generosity of the Sun.*

1. For additional information on the early Universe, matter formation, and the formation of Earth see chap. 1: Water.

Ocean Foam

The ocean covering our young planet was turbulent. For thousands of years violent storms churned the seas. Meteorites bombarded Earth, causing impacts that shook it to its core. Magma beneath the fragile ocean floor shifted and cracked, releasing gases that boiled to the surface. Volcanoes erupted, raining dust and spewing lava into the waters. As the waters swirled and crashed, the elements from the stars came together and pulled apart. In the rocking waves countless compounds were created and destroyed.[2]

For life to form in this unlikely environment it needed a container, a miraculous vessel that could keep life's fragile processes protected as it held needed ingredients in and forced waste products out. This container would balance internal stability with external contact. The miraculous vessels that allowed life to form in this chaos were most likely flimsy films of oil. They were bubbles much like soap bubbles and ocean foam.

As these fragile spheres formed, some of them encased chemical reactions. Once protected from turbulence, these reactions needed a constant flow of chemicals and energy to continue. In time some of the oily membranes developed the ability to allow necessary chemicals to pass in and waste to pass out while still maintaining a barrier to toxins and turbulence. Eventually one of these self-sustaining systems was able to replicate itself, and so "fidgeted to life."[3] From this very first living being, oil has controlled the flow of nutrients and energy through a cell and has protected it from its environment.

Photosynthesis

The first living being may have formed near deep-sea vents 3.8 billion years ago. Within the embrace of their oily membranes these single-celled bacteria adapted to the ocean's depths and then spread toward its surface. A short geological time later the beings near the surface of the oceans began to adapt to light. As they became increasingly comfortable with the Sun they developed photocells (or chloroplasts) that captured

---

2. For a description of the conditions when life formed on Earth see especially chap. 4 in Peter D. Ward and Donald Brownlee, *Rare Earth: Why Complex Life Is Uncommon in the Universe* (New York: Copernicus, 2000).

3. Bill Bryson, *A Short History of Nearly Everything* (New York: Random House, 2003), 293.

sunlight. Fewer than 200 million years after oil first provided cells with membranes, life began to ingest sunlight.[4]

As these photosynthetic beings enjoyed this new energy source the future of the planet changed dramatically. Ultraviolet light from the Sun was destructive to early ocean life. While most life was confined to darkness beneath the reach of ultraviolet light, photosynthetic beings hovered close enough to the surface to absorb sunlight and just deep enough to avoid destruction by the radiation. These resilient creatures developed a way to use sunlight to split water molecules, but used only its hydrogen for fuel. As they did, bubble by bubble the oxygen they released reached the ocean surface and drifted into the atmosphere. As the oxygen ascended, it interacted with ultraviolet light and slowly formed a blanket of ozone. This ozone layer reflected ultraviolet light, bouncing most of it away from Earth and thus keeping it from reaching the fragile life below. Because of this buildup of oxygen that protected Earth, during the next two billion years the surface of the ocean waters became safer, and even the dry land of the emerging continents became habitable for bacterial life.[5]

The increase in oxygen, however, gradually became a threat. As photosynthetic beings split more water molecules and released ever more oxygen, the amount of dissolved oxygen within the oceans became too great for many organisms to tolerate. Some beings may have hid from the new menace by burrowing into bigger hosts. Some may have been engulfed by larger beings. However it happened, a portion of these new combinations formed stable symbiotic relationships, and what were once independent beings became permanent parts of one another. With these new arrangements, Earth's creatures developed surprising new abilities. Soon after oxygen soaked the oceans, multicellularity, respiration, sexual reproduction, and predation entered the world. With predation, the Promethean beings that stole light from the Sun and changed the world forever became prey to be eaten. They became the bottom of the food chain and a source of energy for the rest of the world's creatures.

4. Armand Delsemme, *Our Cosmic Origins: From the Big Bang to the Emergence of Life and Intelligence* (Cambridge: Cambridge University Press, 1998), 238.
5. Ibid., 162.

Land Plants

The story of olives' ancestors continues on a dry beach some 425 million years ago.[6] The ancestor that linked photosynthetic marine life and primitive land plants may have been green algae. Perhaps because they found themselves stranded at low tides, algae began to adapt to the rigors of aridity and gravity. With these adaptations begun in green algae, the plant kingdom was born.[7]

Once plants adapted to life on shore they began to spread across the land, providing habitat that encouraged animals to follow. Bryophytes (such as mosses and liverworts) were followed by arthropods, the earliest animals on land. These shelled and segmented creatures first ventured onto beaches to feast on plankton left behind by tides and then began to thrive in habitats newly prepared by plants. Plants set the table and spread the banquet for life on land. Later, as coastal waterways became lush with ferns, insects of many kinds grew abundant. These were followed by the amphibians, who dined on them. Conifers and other plants that needed less water than ferns moved further inland. Insects, and then lizards, moved with them. When mammals were typically the size of mice these plants provided habitat and their seeds offered a concentrated food source. As plants adapted to different environments and spread across the continents, so did the animals. One hundred twenty-five million years after plants took root on land, vast forests covered the continents. As these forests aged, their decaying matter created the richer soils that flowering plants needed. In many bioregions flowering plants out-competed the conifers for sunlight in the canopy and space on the forest floor. By the beginning of the Cenozoic Era, 65 million years ago, flowering plants dominated the continents.[8]

6. For a poetic telling of the story of plants, see "How Flowers Changed the World," in Loren Eiseley, *The Star Thrower* (New York: Harcourt Brace, 1978).

7. Another theory is that the progenitors of plants are lichens. These plantlike organisms are a composite of algae and fungi. The algae produce energy for the pair through photosynthesis in leaflike parts while the fungi pull nutrients from the surface with primitive roots. In a mutual relationship the fungi gain carbohydrates while the algae gain moisture, mineral nutrients, and stability. See Thomas L. Rost, Michael G. Barbour, C. Ralph Stocking, and Terence M. Murphy, *Plant Biology* (Davis, CA: Wadsworth, 1998), 354.

8. For the complete story of plant evolution see ibid.

Flowering Plants

Flowering plants (such as grasses, rose bushes, and olive trees) thrive because of an exuberant generosity and a radical interdependence.[9] Unlike more primitive plants, which are damaged when their sun-storing leaves, stems, or roots are eaten, flowering plants are able not only to survive the appetites of animals but also to flourish with their help. While earlier plants relied on the randomness of wind and water to carry spores and disperse seeds, generously feeding animals are flowering plants' assurance of reproductive success.[10] To ensure pollination, flowers produce nectar that birds and insects relish. As these animals feed on nectar they carry sticky pollen from the male stamens of one flower to the female style of another.[11] Plants became more likely to exchange pollen within their own species as their pollinators developed specific preferences for particular types of flowers. By this specialized feeding of their pollinators, flowering plants found a more reliable means of fertilization than earlier plants. Through their generous production of nectar and their interdependence with their pollinators, flowering plants are reliably pollinated, and butterflies, moths, bees, ants, hummingbirds, and others are able to feast.

Flowering plants not only produce nectar to feed pollinators; in a surprising reversal they also produce seeds designed to be eaten. In earlier plants the theft of seeds destroyed reproductive success and squandered the energy of the parent plant. In flowering plants the reverse is true. To assure seed dispersal once a plant is pollinated, its flowers mature into succulent fruit.[12] These crafty plants encase their seeds within fruit that is appealing to animals. While the animal feasts on the fruit it ingests the seeds within. Then, as the fruit is digested, the seeds pass through the animal and are deposited at a distance from the parent plant, complete with fertilizer. In fact, some seeds, including olive seeds, will not germinate unless they have passed through an animal's digestive tract, where acids soften the seed case sufficiently to allow it to sprout. Some animals also assist plants by hoarding and burying fruit. Others get seeds tangled

---

9. Flowering plants are angiosperms, all of which bear fruit. For more information on angiosperms see ibid., chap. 25.

10. Delsemme, *Our Cosmic Origins*, 183.

11. Millions of years since plants left the oceans, sperm swim to eggs in flower nectar. For information on angiosperm fertilization see Rost et al., *Plant Biology*, 432–33.

12. Ibid., 425.

in their coats, which they shake loose at different locations. Since animals tend to stay in the same habitat as the fruit they contact, they usually deposit the seeds in a suitable environment for new plants to flourish.

Of course, not all seeds are placed in such a way that they will produce adult plants. As with other species, abundance is crucial to the survival of flowering plants. With a greater abundance of fruit for animals, more seeds are carried to more locations where they will have a chance to grow. Fruit that is not carried away and does not produce new plants is still not wasted. As it decomposes, this fruit enriches the soil community and provides nutrients that feed other plants. So flowering plants thrive at the bottom of the food chain not through ruthless self-protection but through new levels of generosity and interdependence. Of all the flowering plants that grew in the regions of early human civilization, olive trees were among the most fecund.

Olives

To understand the generosity of olives we must pause to look back over the path we have traveled. After more than 13 billion years of cosmic history, 4 billion years of Earth history, and 400 million years of plant history, we finally arrive at olives. In the previous pages we traced the lineage of olive trees from green algae on dry shores to land plants, then to conifers, and finally to flowering plants. We saw that the lineage of olives goes back to the oceans where photosynthesis began, back to the first living beings, back to the stars, and ultimately back to the hydrogen created in the first moments of the Universe. As we now turn our focus to olive trees and olive oil we gather these stories and remember that, like all living beings, olives have oily cell membranes, and like all plants, they are photosynthetic. This Promethean inheritance allows olives to capture the Sun's energy so that they perpetually secure energy for themselves and for the rest of the food chain. Like all fruits, the olive shares in a generosity of interdependence that ensures its own survival as it feeds the animal community. With these stories in mind we turn now to the domestication of olive trees.

Domestication of Olives

For tens of thousands of years several species of wild olives grew throughout the Mediterranean. They ripened in winter and so provided a food source when other vegetation was scarce. Browsing animals, such as goats, and a variety of birds including raven and quail, feasted on olives long before humans began cultivation.

Before humans systematically tended plants, hunter-gatherer cultures harvested olives and squeezed their oil by hanging them in nets. They may have pruned the trees, perhaps first accidentally breaking branches while they harvested the olives and later deliberately as a way to increase the trees' yield.[13] This protoagriculture may have nourished tribal people for thousands of years before farmers began to domesticate olives by replanting and grafting wild olive shoots.[14]

Olive trees were among the earliest to be cultivated, perhaps because they respond readily to human care.[15] A modest amount of attention is enough to restore a failing tree. Orchards deserted for generations regain productivity almost immediately when they are tended again. When trees are healthy, even if they are not tended well, they will produce abundant fruit rich in oil and nutrients. However, when trees are cared for, when, for example, they are pruned to maximize their access to sunlight, they produce even more generously.

Devoted attention to the olives yields the best oil. Because fruit even in the same cluster ripens at different rates, attentive harvesting can involve several weeks of toil in winter weather. This elongated season of ripening is common to flowering plants and ensures that animals are fed over a longer period of time. As the olives are picked at the peak of ripeness, each one is checked for blemishes that might indicate the presence of worms; such olives degrade the flavor of the oil. The gift of these damaged olives, however, is not lost, because their oil can be used for lamps. For the best oil, unblemished olives are pressed as soon as possible after harvesting. Any delay allows time for the olives to bruise and their oil to deteriorate. Once the olives are pressed, the oil is protected from deterioration by being stored in dark containers away from light and heat. Olive oil is ready to use as soon as it is pressed; however, the flavor reaches its peak after a few weeks. When properly stored, olive oil lasts for about a year. With each turn of the seasons olives are tended, harvested, pressed, and ready before the last year's supply runs out.

When animals (including humans) eat olives, they release the sun-energy held in the oil of the ripe fruit into their own bodies. Their metabolism immediately burns some of the oil for energy; some of the oil

13. Rost et al., *Plant Biology*, 423.

14. Mort Rosenblum, *Olives: The Life and Lore of a Noble Fruit* (New York: North Point Press, 1996), 10.

15. Apostolos Kiritsakis, *Olive Oil: From the Tree to the Table*, 2d ed. (Trumbull, CT: Food & Nutrition Press, 1998), 1.

is incorporated into cell membranes and the remainder of this abundant plant oil is stored in fatty tissues. The story of oil continues with its incorporation into the flesh of those who eat it.

Oil in Our Own Bodies

Without our oily cellular membranes we would not hear a baby's cry, feel a lover's touch, or know to pull our hand away from a flame. Oily membranes differentiate the smallest parts of our bodies, govern the flow in and out of each cell, protect our skin, and communicate sensations throughout our bodies. As the boundary of the cell, the membrane defines and differentiates it from its external environment and establishes the cell as the smallest self-organizing unit of the body. When the cell reproduces, the membrane stretches until it splits and re-forms around two distinct daughter cells.

The construction of the cell membrane allows transportation into and out of our cells. The membrane is made of oil embedded with proteins. Cell membranes are semifluid and selectively permeable. As the oil and the protein molecules move around one other they allow small molecules to pass between them. The membrane is selectively permeable; it allows only certain molecules to pass through, based on the needs of the cell.[16]

The oily membranes of our cells allow us to experience a caress and respond with a smile.[17] A sensitivity to electrical charge enables cell membranes to communicate sensations to the entire body. When electrically charged particles such as potassium or sodium are unevenly distributed inside and outside the cell, the membrane becomes polarized. This change in polarization is relayed to all the surrounding cells and they also become polarized. This chain reaction of polarization transmits information throughout the body. Although all living cells spread information, neurons—cells of the nervous system—transmit it very quickly. In addition to having their own cell membranes, most neurons are also bundled in a specialized membrane called a myelin sheath that speeds the chain reaction from the cell throughout the nervous system of the body, helping the body to recognize and respond to the sensations quickly. These membranes carry a chemical message to the brain, which can recognize

16. For information about the structure and function of the cell see especially chap. 6 in Jean P. Milani, Biological Sciences Curriculum Study, et al., *Biological Science: A Molecular Approach*, 6th ed. (Lexington, MA.: D. C. Heath and Company, 1990).

17. For information about the function of the nervous system see especially ibid., chap. 22.

the sensation and initiate an appropriate response. Whether the sensation is that of a loved one's touch or an icy rain, the information our cell membranes relay throughout our bodies allows us to respond.

Our skin is protected by a light sheen of oil. The shine on our faces and the softness of our hands is the result of oil secreted from the multitude of sebaceous glands in our skin. This oil, or sebum (which means "tallow" or "fat" in Latin), is essential to the health of our skin and of the rest of our body. As in cellular membranes, oils in our skin help provide a barrier between the internal and external environment. With the aid of sebum our skin provides a barrier to fluid loss. It also blocks the passage of pathogens into our bodies by keeping the skin lubricated and moist, preventing it from becoming brittle and cracking. Sebum also inhibits the growth of microorganisms on the skin. Additionally, babies are born with their skin coated with a waxy substance called vernix, an oil secreted by their sebaceous glands. Before our birth and throughout our life the oil in our skin protects us and keeps us glowing with health.

All the oil in our bodies derives ultimately from a plant source. Even the oils we obtain through animal sources came into the animal when it was grazing on plants. These oils in plants originate in a complex resonance between sunlight and plants. Through photosynthesis plants capture the Sun's energy and pass it on to us when we consume them. Plants, particularly through oils, mediate the Sun's energy to the rest of the Earth community. As Thomas Berry says, "All life depends on what grass can do."[18]

THE SACRAMENTAL STORY OF OLIVE OIL

The sense of self-giving we see in the natural history of oil continues in the sacramental story. Anointing is the ritualization of the outpouring of the Spirit's presence on a person (or thing) and her or his gift of self in response. This reciprocal giving is made visible by the radiance of olive oil. When something is anointed, it shines. Whether with a person or a liturgical vessel, oil shares its botanical ability to interact with light and with the anointed. The oil itself does not remain visible; rather, its radiance spreads across the one being honored.

18. Emma Morris and Jane Zipp, eds., "Universe as Story," in *Thomas Berry: The Great Story*, DVD, directed by Nancy Stetson and Penny Morrell (Oley, PA: Bullfrog Films, 2002).

The sacramental story of olive oil shimmers with joy. Oil—unlike water or fire—has no judgmental or punishing aspect. No floods or drowning, no furnaces or testing enter oil's story. As we shall see in the biblical stories and blessings of olive oil that follow, anointing with oil is a cause for joy. Ritual anointing sets people and things apart and announces their identity as consecrated beings dedicated to the divine. The presence of oil, whether by miracle or by design, is a sign of faithfulness and God's blessing. Even in exorcism and the sacrament of the sick, oil is a cause for joy. Oil used in these rituals gives strength and restoration; it only peripherally involves remission of sin. Perhaps the joy in olive oil's story is most brilliant when the presence of the Holy Spirit is called the "oil of gladness."

Olive Oil's Biblical Source

Old Testament

> *Loving and Living God, we rejoice*
> *in your gift of Oil for baptism,*
> *Oil that glistened on Aaron's face and beard,*
> *and whose miraculous abundance*
> *we celebrate at Chanukah.*
> *Oil of widows and bridesmaids, radiant with fidelity.*

Olive trees and olive oil permeated ancient Hebrew culture. Not only did an olive tree represent the Tree of Life in the center of the Garden of Eden; an olive branch in the beak of a dove represented the restoration of life to Noah in the ark. Olive oil was a source of nutrition, a sign of abundance, a symbol of wisdom, and a cause for joy.[19] Olive oil served both household and sacred purposes. Its many uses included bathing, cooking, cleaning, cosmetics, lubrication, fuel, healing, and anointing. Olive oil was also a preservative. Fruit and cheese could be stored in jars of oil, and metal tools were rubbed with oil to prevent rusting and corrosion. Olive oil was a trading commodity and a sign of wealth. If a family had only one olive tree it would not be poor. The use of olive oil in healing both physical and demonic illnesses revealed the physical and spiritual

---

19. For a complete discussion of the ancient and biblical uses of oil see Gerhard Kittel, Geoffrey W. Bromiley, and Gerhard Friedrich, *Theological Dictionary of the New Testament* (Grand Rapids: Eerdmans, 1964), esp. 2:470–72.

efficacy of the oil. In its use to light lamps and in anointing, olive oil was a symbol of God's presence.

The most celebratory use of olive oil was anointing. Anointing was commonly used for bodily comfort, joyful celebration, and as a sign of honor shown to a guest. Olive oil, sometimes mixed with fragrances, was used in rituals to anoint kings, priests, high priests, prophets, or objects employed in worship. These anointings were variously acts of commissioning by God, rites of dedication and purification, or celebrations of God's conferral of the Spirit for a specific task.

In spite of the many uses of olive oil, it does not flow ubiquitously through Scripture the way water does. Biblical literature reflects a desert community's appreciation of water. Water was precious and sometimes scarce. Concern with the fluctuating shortage and abundance of water, its destructive floods and its life-sustaining wells, are central to many biblical stories. By contrast, olive oil was generally abundant in the land of Israel. As essential as it was to almost every aspect of life, its continual presence allowed it to remain almost invisible. Unlike water, whose moods draw our attention, the simple generosity of oil often remains in the background even as it shines light on the central message of the story.

Aaron's Anointing

While the Israelites wandered through the desert after their Exodus from Egypt, God chose Aaron and his descendants to be priests. When Moses returns from the mountain with the Ten Commandments, the people construct a tabernacle and tent to house the sacred tablets. After the Tent of Meeting is completed and furnished with an altar, lampstands, and various utensils as God has ordered, Aaron is anointed priest. In a lavish celebration Aaron and all the furnishings of the Tent of Meeting are made radiant with God's blessing through a sumptuous anointing with olive oil.

> The LORD spoke to Moses, saying: "Take Aaron and his sons with him, the vestments, the anointing oil, the bull of sin offering, the two rams, and the basket of unleavened bread; and assemble the whole congregation at the entrance of the tent of meeting."
> . . .
> Then Moses brought Aaron and his sons forward, and washed them with water. He put the tunic on him, fastened the sash around him, clothed him with the robe, and put the ephod on him.
> . . .

Then Moses took the anointing oil and anointed the tabernacle and all that was in it, and consecrated them. He sprinkled some of it on the altar seven times, and anointed the altar and all its utensils, and the basin and its base, to consecrate them. He poured some of the anointing oil on Aaron's head and anointed him, to consecrate him. (Leviticus 8:1-3, 6-7, 10-12)

This is the first account of an anointing of a priest, prophet, or king in the Old Testament. This priestly anointing is accompanied by the anointing of the objects used in worship, or sacramentals. The fullness of God's blessing is manifest in the copious amount of oil used to anoint Aaron as well as all the ritual objects and the altar. Indeed, the altar is anointed seven times. In the desert sun everything in the sacred tent glistens with God's blessing.[20] The exuberant anointing of Aaron also appears in the Psalms. We read:

> How very good and pleasant it is
>   when kindred live together in unity!
> It is like the precious oil on the head,
>   running down upon the beard,
> on the beard of Aaron,
>   running down over the collar of his robes.
> It is like the dew of Hermon,
>   which falls on the mountains of Zion.
> For there the Lord ordained his blessing,
>   life forevermore. (Psalm 133)

This psalm of David celebrates the goodness of a close community (and perhaps the return of the exiles from Babylon). It compares this goodness to the life-giving waters of snow-capped Mount Hermon and to the overflowing oil of Aaron's anointing. This blessing is expressed as an excessive overabundance of olive oil. The image of oil shining on Aaron's face, beard, and clothes evokes a sense of joyful celebration and laughter.

---

20. We notice that as part of this joyful celebration Aaron is ritually washed in water prior to the anointing with oil. This testifies to the ancient history of the baptismal sequence of purification in water followed by a conferral of blessing made visible by oil.

Elisha and the Widow's Oil

Our second story, Elisha and the Widow's Oil, is recorded in the second book of Kings. A recurring theme in 1 and 2 Kings is fidelity to God: the faithful ultimately prosper, but the unfaithful suffer the consequence of their infidelity. In the midst of stories of kings and wars, 2 Kings pauses to tell some of the miracles of the prophet Elisha. In this story God rewards the faithfulness of a prophet and his widow by ransoming their children with olive oil.

> Now the wife of a member of the company of prophets cried to Elisha, "Your servant my husband is dead; and you know that your servant feared the Lord, but a creditor has come to take my two children as slaves." Elisha said to her, "What shall I do for you? Tell me, what do you have in the house?" She answered, "Your servant has nothing in the house, except a jar of oil." He said, "Go outside, borrow vessels from all your neighbors, empty vessels and not just a few. Then go in, and shut the door behind you and your children, and start pouring into all these vessels; when each is full, set it aside." So she left him and shut the door behind her and her children; they kept bringing vessels to her, and she kept pouring. When the vessels were full, she said to her son, "Bring me another vessel." But he said to her, "There are no more." Then the oil stopped flowing. She came and told the man of God, and he said, "Go sell the oil and pay your debts, and you and your children can live on the rest." (2 Kings 4:1-7)

Olive oil is all this desperate widow still has in her home. Through this small jar of oil, God's compassion pours out and saves the children of the faith-filled widow from slavery. Moreover, the lavish abundance of the oil, which fills every jar, provides an income for the grieving family. This story shows oil as a valued commodity as well as a medium for God's blessing.

In a similar story, recounted in 1 Kings, God sends the prophet Elijah to a widow in Zarephath during a drought. When he meets her, the widow is collecting sticks for a fire so that she can make a few cakes with the last of her flour and oil. After she and her son eat, they will die because they have nothing else. On hearing her story, Elijah asks to share their meal and prophesies, saying: "The jar of meal will not be emptied and the jug of oil will not fail until the day that the LORD sends rain on the earth" (1 Kgs 17:14). And it was as Elijah said: neither jar of meal nor jug of oil emptied. The primary purpose of these two stories and other parallel accounts in 1 and 2 Kings is to establish Elisha as Elijah's successor. Nonetheless, in both stories the abundance of olive oil serves as the means of God's blessing. Without oil the widows and the children would be lost.

The Story of Chanukah

An abundance of olive oil is also central to the story of Chanukah. The miracle of the oil of Chanukah is not told in the Old Testament, but it is part of Jewish tradition, rooted in the stories of the purification of the temple in Jerusalem. As told in the First and Second Books of Maccabees, by the middle of the second century BCE the Jews of Jerusalem had lost favor with God. Their kings protected neither people nor temple. Gentiles, with Jews as accomplices, sacked and desecrated the temple. In the account in 2 Maccabees, in the midst of civil unrest Judas Maccabaeus, with the help of God, recruits a small band of faithful Jews who drive out the Gentiles and restore the temple.

> Now Maccabaeus and his followers, the Lord leading them on, recovered the temple and the city; they tore down the altars that had been built in the public square by the foreigners, and also destroyed the sacred precincts. They purified the sanctuary, and made another altar of sacrifice; then, striking fire out of flint, they offered sacrifices, after a lapse of two years, and they offered incense and lighted lamps and set out the bread of the Presence. When they had done this, they fell prostrate and implored the Lord that they might never again fall into such misfortunes, but that, if they should ever sin, they might be disciplined by him with forbearance and not be handed over to blasphemous and barbarous nations. It happened that on the same day on which the sanctuary had been profaned by the foreigners, the purification of the sanctuary took place, that is, on the twenty-fifth day of the same month, which was Chislev. They celebrated it for eight days with rejoicing, in the manner of the festival of booths, remembering how not long before, during the festival of booths, they had been wandering in the mountains and caves like wild animals. Therefore, carrying ivy-wreathed wands and beautiful branches and also fronds of palm, they offered hymns of thanksgiving to him who had given success to the purifying of his own holy place. They decreed by public edict, ratified by vote, that the whole nation of the Jews should observe these days every year. (2 Maccabees 10:1-8)

The legend of Chanukah (which means consecration) tells us that as the Maccabees cleaned and restored the temple they searched for ritually pure oil needed for the rededication. They found, hidden away, a small flask of oil untouched by the Gentiles. It was hardly enough to give light for one day. Miraculously, this unlikely amount of olive oil burned for eight days, giving those faithful to God ample time to harvest, press, and bless a new supply of oil. As in the anointing of Aaron, all the furnishings and utensils of the temple were consecrated once again and dedicated to sacred service. The unfailing generosity of olive oil expresses God's desire and provision for the restoration of the temple and of those who remain faithful.

In each of these stories from the Old Testament, God's blessing is shown through the exuberant generosity of olive oil. Aaron shines with the oil that marks him and everything in the tent as dedicated to God; the widows and their children are saved though a miraculous abundance of oil; a small flask of oil shines brightly in the temple long enough for the faithful to press new oil for the celebration of the temple's consecration and rededication. These stories move from celebration to despair and back to celebration. It is as if Aaron's joy is hidden away in the small jars of oil, the last drops of hope that swell into the life-giving, restorative joy of God's presence, the oil of gladness.

New Testament

> *Loving and Living God, we rejoice*
> *in your gift of Oil for baptism,*
> *Oil of widows and bridesmaids, radiant with fidelity*
> *Oil of anointing, presence of God made visible*
> *hovering over the waters of creation,*
> *bearing the olive branch to Noah after the flood,*
> *appearing above the Jordan to announce*
> *Jesus as your beloved.*

As in the Old Testament, olive oil has a significant, though infrequent, presence in the New Testament. Like the Hebrews before them, the Christian writers were immersed in an olive culture where the everydayness of olive oil allowed it to be taken for granted and remain mostly invisible. Along with its household uses, olive oil was employed for physical and spiritual healing.[21] Other than serving as a curative ointment, olive oil is mentioned in two New Testament narratives and alluded to in two others.

The Parable of the Ten Bridesmaids

The Parable of the Ten Bridesmaids is the only story in the New Testament in which olive oil is prominently featured. In this story, possessing enough oil to keep their lamps lit allows the wise bridesmaids entrance into a wedding celebration. As part of Matthew's eschatological discourse, this parable teaches about what is required to enter into the reign of God. In the story Jesus warns his listeners of the coming destruction of the temple in Jerusalem, the advent of the last days, and the final judgment. Jesus' message is one of warning and caution, advising his disciples to be ready.

> Then the kingdom of heaven will be like this. Ten bridesmaids took their lamps and went to meet the bridegroom. Five of them were foolish, and five were wise. When the foolish took their lamps, they took no oil with them; but the wise took flasks of oil with their lamps. As the bridegroom was delayed, all of them became drowsy and slept. But at midnight, there was a shout, "Look! Here is the bridegroom! Come out to meet him." Then all those bridesmaids got up and trimmed their lamps. The foolish said to the wise, "Give us some of your oil, for our lamps are going out." But the wise replied, "No! There will not be enough for you and for us; you had better go to the dealers and buy some for yourselves." And while they went to buy it, the bridegroom came, and those who were ready went with him into the wedding banquet; and the door was shut. Later the other bridesmaids came also, saying, "Lord, lord, open to us." But he replied, "Truly I tell you, I do not know you." Keep awake therefore, for you know neither the day nor the hour. (Matthew 25:1-13)

Greeting the bridegroom with a bright lamp is required for the bridesmaids to enter the banquet. Only half the bridesmaids are prepared for the long wait. Perhaps they had waited for this groom before and knew he was likely to be late. Perhaps they would not take the chance of missing his arrival. Whatever the cause, the oil they carry shows their dedication to the bridegroom.

---

21. For examples of the healing use of olive oil in the New Testament see the parable of the Good Samaritan (Luke 10:34), the exorcism of demons (Mark 6:13), and anointing of the sick (Jas 5:14).

That the wise bridesmaids do not run out of oil calls to mind the Old Testament's widows as well as the flask of Chanukah oil hidden in the defiled temple. The abundance of oil suggests that these maidens, like the widows, were faithful and so had God's favor. As with the temple oil, a small flask is there when most needed. In both the earlier stories and this parable, oil symbolizes faithfulness to God; it is the narrative evidence of one's fidelity, one's perseverance in relationship to God. Moreover, it is interesting to notice that only a small flask is needed.

Oil of Gladness

In the story of the oil of gladness, the author of the letter to the Hebrews offers the overflowing anointing with the oil of gladness as evidence that the Son of God is greater even than the angels. Relying on passages from the Psalms to strengthen his point, he writes:

> For to which of the angels did God ever say,
>   "You are my Son;
>   today I have begotten you"? [Ps 2:7]
> Or again,
>   "I will be his Father,
>   and he will be my Son"? [Ps 2:7]
> And again, when he brings the firstborn into the world, he says,
>   "Let all God's angels worship him." [Ps 97:7]
> Of the angels he says,
>   "He makes his angels winds,
>   and his servants flames of fire." [Ps 104:4]
> But of the Son he says,
>   "Your throne, O God, is forever and ever,
>   and the righteous scepter is the scepter of your kingdom.
>   You have loved righteousness and hated wickedness;
>   therefore God, your God, has anointed you
>   with the oil of gladness beyond your companions." [Ps 45:7]
>   (Hebrews 1:5-9)

The Bible, both Old and New Testaments, contains only three references to the oil of gladness. In the first reference, Psalm 45, Aaron's anointing—in which oil flows over his head, down his beard, and into his cloak—is likened to a snow-capped mountain and to the joy of living in a close community. In the second reference, Isaiah 61, God's Anointed One brings deliverance to the people. He "gives them a garland instead of ashes, the oil of gladness instead of mourning." Joy in the presence of God is symbolized as oil, oil the Anointed One gives to others. In the final reference, quoted above, the Son is the one dripping oil. He is anointed with the oil of gladness beyond all others. Both Aaron, the first priest, and Jesus the priest, prophet, king, and Son, are anointed with the oil of gladness. Jesus the Christ gives this gift of the oil of gladness to those who follow him. Indeed, within a few decades of his death Jesus' followers were called Christians because they shared in the Christ's anointing.

The Anointing at Bethany

In Mark, Matthew, and John's gospel, the story of the anointing of Jesus takes place at Bethany a few days before Passover. In Luke, an anointing occurs earlier in Jesus' mission in the home of Simon the Pharisee. While there are differences in these stories, in each case Jesus accepts the woman's extraordinary gift and rebukes those who criticize her. Although not mentioned in the English translation of this story, the Greek translation and Jewish custom make it clear that olive oil is the medium of the perfumed unction.[22] In the earliest of the gospel, we read:

> While he was at Bethany in the house of Simon the leper, as he sat at the table, a woman came with an alabaster jar of very costly ointment of nard, and she broke open the jar and poured the ointment on his head. But some were there who said to one another in anger, "Why was the ointment wasted in this way? For this ointment could have been sold for more than three hundred denarii, and the money given to the poor." And they scolded her. But Jesus said, "Let her alone; why do you trouble her? She has performed a good service for me. For you always have the poor with you, and you can show kindness to them whenever you wish; but you will not always have me. She has done what she could; she has anointed my body beforehand for its burial. Truly I tell you, wherever the good news is proclaimed in the whole world, what she has done will be told in remembrance of her." (Mark 14:3-9)

This lavish anointing brings to mind the excessive amount of oil used in Aaron's consecration to priesthood. Through it, the woman of Bethany ritually prepares Jesus for his mission to preach in Jerusalem as well as

22. I am grateful to Dr. Luzia Sutter-Rehmann for allowing me to read her forthcoming essay, "Trustworthy of Suspicious: Debating Olive Oil in Second-Temple Judaism and the Anointing of Jesus," which deepened my knowledge of the customs regarding olive oil in ancient Israel.

for its likely outcome. Although in this reading olive oil is eclipsed by costly nard, oil is the base ingredient of the ointment. Without ritually pure olive oil handled by a trustworthy agent, the anointing would be suspect, as it was in the story of the anointing in the home of Simon the Pharisee. Even then, Jesus accepted the fragrant oil and the loving attention of the sinful woman, rejecting laws that limited her from full table fellowship. The luxuriant fragrance of the nard eventually dissipates into the surrounding air, but the story of the anointing made possible by olive oil and the gift of these women will be told forever.

The Garden of Gethsemane

In the story of the Garden of Gethsemane Jesus knows he is soon to be betrayed as he celebrates the Passover with his disciples. After the meal Jesus leads them to the Mount of Olives. When he reaches "the place" (the place of prayer, the place where he will be tested to the limits of his endurance), he says to them, "Pray that you may not come into the time of trial."

> Then he withdrew from them about a stone's throw, knelt down, and prayed, "Father, if you are willing, remove this cup from me; yet, not my will but yours be done." Then an angel from heaven appeared to him and gave him strength. In his anguish he prayed more earnestly, and his sweat became like great drops of blood falling down on the ground. (Luke 22:39-44)

In this brief story we see Jesus crushed in agony as he first pleads with God to spare him and then accepts a cruel death. Like the water that flows from Jesus' side and blesses the Earth at Calvary, here at Gethsemane sweat is pressed out of the Anointed One and falls to the Earth like blood. Perhaps Earth's anointing with the sweat of Jesus' agony foreshadows the blessing that would eventually come from Jesus' obedient surrender to God's will. In this anointing of Jesus' faithful obedience and sweat, the agony of Thursday becomes the joy of Sunday. Luke's narrative suggests an image of Jesus crushed like an olive. Not only does this story take place on the Mount of Olives, but in the Garden of Gethsemane, which means olive press.

✝ ✝ ✝ ✝✝ ✝

More stories of olive oil could be told. There are stories of kings and riches. There are stories of offerings and healings, as well as stories of bread and lamps and wisdom and seduction. In each of these stories oil is a cause for joy and a sign of abundance. Olive oil is a domestic staple of biblical life that draws no attention to itself but glows with God's generosity. The Christian baptismal tradition of anointing radiates from the Biblical stories of oil. In the following section we watch the radiance spread through the patristic and contemporary understandings of anointing at baptism.

OLIVE OIL IN THE BAPTISMAL TRADITION

Loving and Living God, we rejoice
in your gift of Oil for baptism,
Oil of baptism that heals and seals us in your love.

Now that we have recalled the key moments in the natural history, and biblical stories of oil, we turn to the baptismal tradition itself. From there we follow the story of oil in the baptismal rites as it is expressed in blessings of oil and instructions to candidates for baptism from the early centuries of the church to the seventh-century Gelasian Sacramentary.[23] This part of oil's story concludes with the current teachings in the *Catechism* and the Rite of Christian Initiation for Adults.

Patristic Understanding of Olive Oil in Baptism

In the biblical and Christian traditions anointing with olive oil is the ritual acknowledgment of the anointing of the Holy Spirit. In the anointing of Aaron we saw fragrant olive oil used to signify the spiritual anointing of Aaron as priest. Additionally, the anointing of the furnishings of the Tent of Meeting proclaimed that they were reserved for ritual use. In the story of Jesus' baptism he was publicly anointed with the Spirit. After Jesus came out of the water the Spirit descended on him visibly in the form of a dove, and God's voice announced Jesus as God's son, the Beloved. Since the early days of the church, olive oil has been used in baptism to make visible the invisible anointing of the Spirit.

---

23. H. A. Wilson, ed., *The Gelasian Sacramentary: Liber Sacramentorum Romanae Ecclesiae* (Oxford: Clarendon Press, 1894).

As was done in the previous chapter for water, we turn now to the teaching of the church fathers to continue our story of olive oil and anointing. We begin with Kilian McDonnell's retrieval of the cosmic significance of Jesus' anointing and then look with Paul Palmer at anointing in the early baptismal rites of the church.

Significance of Jesus' Anointing at Baptism

From McDonnell's thorough treatment of the cosmic import of the anointing of Jesus at his baptism,[24] we limit our focus to the most significant insights of three teachers: Irenaeus of Lyons, Jacob of Serugh, and Tertullian. Irenaeus (d. 202), who developed one of the most extensive teachings on anointing, writes of two anointings of the Spirit. In the first, God anoints the Word with the Spirit at the beginning of time and anoints and adorns all things through the Christ. The first lines of John's gospel are well known:

> In the beginning was the Word, and the Word was with God, and the Word was God. He was in the beginning with God. All things came into being through him, and without him not one thing came into being. (John 1:1-3)

Similarly, the christological hymn in the letter to the Colossians tells us:

> [Christ] is the image of the invisible God, the firstborn of all creation, for in him all things in heaven and on earth were created, things visible and invisible, whether thrones or dominions or rulers or powers—all things have been created through him and for him. He himself is before all things, and in him all things hold together. (Col 1:15-17)

Irenaeus, John, and Paul tell us that Christ, the Word of God, existed with God before the beginning of creation. Irenaeus notices that "Christ" means "the Anointed" and that, through the anointed Word, God brings into existence and anoints all of creation. Perhaps reflecting on Aaron's radiance and the luster of sacred objects coated with oil, Irenaeus uses the word "adorn" to suggest that the world was not only created, but also beautifully ordered through this anointing.

24. Kilian McDonnell, *The Baptism of Jesus in the Jordan: The Trinitarian and Cosmic Order of Salvation* (Collegeville, MN: Liturgical Press, 1996).

In the second anointing Irenaeus describes, God anoints Jesus with the Spirit at his baptism. Although, Irenaeus explains, Jesus was divine from the moment of his conception and so already possessed the Spirit, at his baptism the human aspect of Jesus received the anointing of the Spirit. This anointing was not for Jesus' benefit, but for the good of humanity and creation. As the Spirit became accustomed to dwelling in the human flesh of Jesus, the presence of the Spirit was mediated to all of humanity.[25] Moreover, since all of creation shares in one relationship with God, all creation received the second anointing of the Spirit through Jesus. According to Irenaeus, at his baptism the Spirit descended on Jesus and radiated through the medium of his flesh to the rest of creation.

Turning now to our second teacher, McDonnell tells us that Jacob of Serugh (ca. 451–521) believed that the significance of Jesus' baptism was not in the washing with water, but in the anointing with the Spirit.[26] In the anointing of the Spirit, Jesus was shown to be Christ, the anointed of God. Recall the first creation story in Genesis: the Spirit moves across the water, God creates a new day and then proclaims it good. Likewise, at his baptism Jesus comes out of the water, the Spirit descends in the form of a dove, and a heavenly voice proclaims Jesus the beloved on whom God's favor rests. The proclamation that accompanied Jesus' anointing made Jesus visible as the Messiah. According to Jacob, those with eyes of faith could see Jesus as the Anointed One and decide to follow him.

The significance of Jesus' anointing has personal as well as universal import. Our third teacher, Tertullian, writes in his *Apology* (ca. 197) that Jesus' followers take the name Christian (those anointed) from the verb to anoint and not from Jesus' title, the Christ. Christians share in the same anointing Jesus received at the Jordan and therefore become christs.[27] This anointing, which refers to kindness and sweetness, invites and challenges all those who see Jesus as the Christ to be visible christs as well, to live their faith publicly with generosity and joy.

Instructions and Blessings of Olive Oil

As we turn from the cosmic significance of Jesus' anointing to instructions and blessings of oil, we notice that Aaron's joy shimmers throughout the baptismal tradition of anointing. We glimpse this joy in Hippolytus, who names the oil used for anointing at baptism the Oil of Thanksgiving,

25. Ibid., 119.
26. Ibid.
27. Ibid., 114.

and again in Cyril of Jerusalem, who teaches that baptismal oil is a symbol of Christ's bounty, and finally in Ephrem the Syrian, who insists that once a person is sealed in chrism she or he can never be lost to God. Even the anointing with the oil of exorcism before baptism shines with joy since its primary purpose is to make the candidate invincible to evil spirits. The sacramental story of anointing with oil shines with joy, favor, and abundance. These themes of joy glisten time and again in Paul Palmer's magnificent collection *Sacraments and Worship*, in which he gathers the extant sacramental instructions, blessings, and liturgies of the early church.[28]

The first extant reference to olive oil and baptism describes the use of two oils in baptism. In a rite recorded in the *Apostolic Tradition* of Hippolytus (ca. 215), two separate oils are used for anointing.[29] In preparation for baptism a bishop first gives thanks over the Oil of Thanksgiving. He then takes a second flask of oil and "exorcize[s] over it." No further elaboration of either the blessing or the exorcism of the oil is extant. Candidates for baptism are anointed first with the Oil of Exorcism while the bishop says, "Let all evil spirits depart far from thee." After the exorcism the candidates enter the water to be washed. When they come out of the water they are anointed with the Oil of Thanksgiving in the name of Jesus Christ.

In the "Hymns on Oil and the Olive," Ephrem the Syrian (ca. 306–373) teaches that anointing leaves an indelible imprint on the baptized. He writes, "For the Holy Spirit uses oil to impress his seal upon his sheep. Just as a ring impresses its signet in wax, so in baptism the seal of the spirit is impressed through oil."[30] As a king uses a ring to mark a document as irrefutably his, so the Spirit marks the baptized. It is not possible to wash off the oil of baptism with water or sin. This is the first extant reference in the ancient texts to the indelible character that baptism confers. Augustine develops this concept, insisting that baptism can only be received once because nothing can erase God's seal.

In his lectures to the newly baptized, Cyril of Jerusalem (ca. 315–386) spoke of Jesus Christ as the good olive tree.[31] In his community the persons to be baptized were first "anointed with oil that had been exorcised, from

28. Paul F. Palmer, ed., *Sacraments and Worship: Liturgy and Doctrinal Development of Baptism, Confirmation, and the Eucharist*, Sources of Christian Theology 1 (Westminster, MD: Newman Press, 1955).

29. Ibid., 6, 7.

30. Ibid., 86.

31. Ibid. All of the quotations referring to Cyril of Jerusalem are taken from Palmer, *Sacraments and Worship*, 13–15.

the hairs of [their] heads to the soles of [their] feet." In so doing, they became "partakers of the good olive-tree, Jesus Christ. For cut off from the wild olive [they] were grafted into the good olive, and were made to share in the prosperity of the true olive-tree." Olive oil was "a symbol of participation in Christ's bounty." Through the invocation of God the oil received "power great enough not only to burn and cleanse all trace of sin, but also to put to flight all the unseen powers of the evil spirit." Cyril then compared the physical anointing with oil that the baptized received to the spiritual anointing with the oil of gladness that Jesus received. He told the newly baptized that they had been anointed with the same Spirit who is the author of all spiritual gladness, and through it they have been made "partakers and associates of Christ." While visible oil anointed the body, the invisible Spirit sanctified the soul. Having received the same anointing as Christ, they became images of Christ.

From these early insights we turn to the Gelasian Sacramentary, the earliest document to give a detailed account of the baptismal ceremony as well as the catechumenate process. Although composed in the seventh or early eighth century, the Gelasian Sacramentary draws on practices that had long been part of Christian tradition. In the Sacramentary we read that in the fourth week of Lent candidates for baptism present themselves to the bishop for exorcism. In this rite the bishop prays six times, three times over the women and three times over the men, addressing the devil and commanding him to flee. The bishop then dips his thumb in exorcised oil and traces a cross on the forehead of each person to be baptized. After this anointing he prays that God "may be pleased to enlighten them with the light of Thy wisdom."

The olive oil used in baptism, as well as in the rite of confirmation, holy orders, and the anointing of the sick, is blessed annually during the Chrism Mass on the Thursday of Holy Week. The chrism—the oil of priests, prophets, and kings—is mixed with fragrance and then blessed. After giving thanks to God, the prayer of blessing from the Gelasian Sacramentary continues:

> . . . in the beginning,
> among the other gifts of Thy bountiful mercy, [thou]
> didst command the earth to put forth fruit-bearing trees.

> Among these there sprang the olive,
> which ministers this rich oily liquid,
> the fruit of which was to serve for sacred chrism.

For David with a prophet's vision
foresaw the sacraments of Thy grace,
and exhorted us to gladden our countenances with oil.

And when the sins of the world had been wiped out by the flood,
it was by bringing an olive branch that a dove
announced that peace had returned to earth
thus offering an image of the future gift.
And all this has been made clear
by visible effects in these latter days when,
after the waters of baptism have washed away all stains of sin,
the anointing with this oil makes our faces glad and peaceful.

Thereafter, to Moses Thy servant, as well,
Thou gavest the command that he should ordain his brother
a priest by anointing him with this ointment
after he had been first washed in water.

And to this anointing came a far greater honor
when your Son, our Lord Jesus Christ,
required John to baptize him in the waters of the Jordan,
so that by sending down upon him the Holy Spirit in the likeness of
a dove and by the witness of the voice then heard,
you might show him to be your only Son in whom you were well
pleased. And so you most clearly proved that he it was
of whom David the prophet had sung,
that he might be anointed with the oil of gladness
above all his companions.

And so, we beseech Thee, holy Lord, Father almighty, eternal God,
to be pleased to consecrate with thy blessing
the rich oil of this creature,
and to commingle therewith the efficacy of the holy Spirit,
through the power of thy Christ,
from whose holy name chrism has taken its name,
with which thou hast anointed priests, kings, prophets,
and Thy martyrs,
that it may be the chrism of salvation
to those who shall be born of water and the Holy Spirit,
and that Thou may make them partakers of the eternal life

and sharers in the glory of heaven.
Through the same Jesus Christ thy Son, our Lord. Amen.[32]

A few days later, on Holy Saturday at the Easter Vigil, chrism stands ready beside the baptismal font. The newly baptized come out of the water and the seven gifts of the Spirit are evoked upon them. The bishop prays:

> Almighty God, Father of our Lord Jesus Christ,
> who hast regenerated Thy servants from water and the Holy Spirit,
> and who hast granted them the remission of all their sins,
> do Thou, Lord, send down upon them the Holy Spirit,
> Thy Comforter, and give them the spirit of wisdom
> and understanding, the spirit of counsel and fortitude,
> the spirit of knowledge and piety;
> fill them with the spirit of fear of God
> in the name of our Lord Jesus Christ,
> with whom Thou livest and reignest always with the Holy Spirit,
> world without end. Amen.[33]

After the prayer, the bishop dips his thumb into the blessed oil and, anointing the newly baptized on the forehead, he says, "The sign of Christ unto eternal life." With the baptismal rite concluded, the bishop proclaims the beginning of the Gloria and then continues the celebration of the Paschal Mass.

This prayer joyously recounts the use of olive oil for anointing. After the world is cleansed by floodwaters, a dove brings an olive branch to Noah as a gift of peace. The prayer tells us that as the baptized come out of the waters they are made radiant with God's joy through anointing. Similarly, the psalmist in the name of David rejoices that God has furnished us with "oil to make the face shine."[34] We are also reminded that the oil blessed through this prayer is the oil of gladness that Christ received beyond all others. Those anointed with oil share in the olive branch given to Noah and in the oil of gladness poured over priests, prophets, and kings, but

---

32. Paul F. Palmer, ed., *Sacraments and Worship: Liturgy and Doctrinal Development of Baptism, Confirmation, and the Eucharist*, Sources of Christian Theology 1 (Westminster, MD: Newman Press, 1955), 35.

33. Ibid., 33–34.

34. Psalm 104:15.

especially over the Christ. Joy, radiance, and richness are the attributes of olive oil celebrated in this prayer.

This blessing, however, recounts only a small portion of the gifts of olive oil. There is no mention of oil in lamps or cooking, in commerce or cleansing, or even in offerings or purification. As suggested previously, perhaps because this prayer was written within the context of an olive-oil culture the significance and uses of olive oil were so apparent they eluded attention. Oil has a hidden generosity, a demureness. Even as it provides nurturance and light to others, oil itself remains in shadow.

As mentioned in the previous chapter on water, the prayers of the Gelasian Sacramentary were used with only minor changes for hundreds of years from the eighth century until the liturgical reforms of Vatican II in the late twentieth century.[35] As we shall see from a comparison of the blessings of oil in the Gelasian and the current Sacramentary, the meaning of oil has not been expanded upon since the Gelasian Sacramentary was written. As was the case with the water, the ancient and current blessings of oil are remarkably similar. Although much scholastic conversation concerned the metaphysics of matter, the attributes of particular sacramentals were not of interest. The similarity of the blessings reflects the absence of further development of the significance of oil. For that reason we continue the sacramental story of olive oil with the current blessing of oil at the Chrism Mass, prayers of baptismal anointing, and the instructions to candidates for baptism found in *The Rites of the Catholic Church*.[36]

Contemporary Understanding of Olive Oil in Baptism

Each year in a festive Mass the olive oil to be used sacramentally in the coming year is blessed by the bishop of the diocese.[37] This Chrism Mass

35. For a side-by-side comparison of the baptismal liturgy in the Gelasian Sacramentary and the 1888 Roman Pontifical see ibid., 25–37.

36. *The Rites of the Catholic Church*, vol. 1 (Collegeville, MN: Liturgical Press, 1990).

37. In this liturgy the bishop blesses three urns of olive oil for the sacramental use of the diocese. One is the Oil of Catechumens, with which those who are investigating the Catholic faith and intent on initiation are anointed. This oil may also be used to anoint infants at the beginning of a baptismal ceremony. This same oil is the Oil of Exorcism first described in the *Apostolic Tradition of Hippolytus* (ca. 215). The second oil is the Oil of the Sick, which is used to restore health, both physical and spiritual, in the sacrament of the sick. The third oil is the chrism used for baptism, confirmation, and holy orders. This is the oil of gladness that carries the presence of the Holy Spirit.

is celebrated during Holy Week, often on the morning of Holy Thursday. After the Mass the newly blessed oils are carried to each parish, where any oil remaining from the previous year is burned. During the Easter Vigil the oils are ceremoniously processed into the church and placed in the sanctuary. The following prayer is the blessing of the oil used for baptism at the Chrism Mass. Notice the themes of radiance and joy that flow through the prayer.

God our maker,
source of all growth in holiness,
accept the joyful thanks and praise
we offer in the name of your Church.

In the beginning, at your command,
the earth produced fruit-bearing trees.
From the fruit of the olive tree
you have provided us with oil for holy chrism.
The prophet David sang of the life and joy
that the oil would bring us in the sacrament of your love.
After the avenging flood,
the dove returning to Noah with an olive branch
announced your gift of peace.
This was a sign of a greater gift to come.
Now the waters of baptism wash away the sins of men,
and by the anointing with olive oil
you make us radiant with your joy.

At your command,
Aaron was washed with water,
and your servant Moses, his brother,
anointed him priest.
This too foreshadowed greater things to come.
After your Son, Jesus Christ our Lord,
asked John for baptism in the waters of Jordan,
you sent the Spirit upon him
in the form of a dove,
and by the witness of your own voice
you declared him your only, well-beloved Son.
In this you clearly fulfilled the prophecy of David,
that Christ would be anointed with the oil of gladness
beyond his fellow men.

And so, Father, we ask you to bless + this oil you have created.
Fill it with the power of your Holy Spirit
through Christ your Son.
It is from this that chrism takes its name
and with chrism you have anointed
for yourself priests and kings,
prophets and martyrs.

Make this chrism a sign of life and salvation
for those who are to be born again in the waters of baptism.
Wash away the evil they have inherited from sinful Adam,
and when they are anointed with this holy oil
make them temples of your glory,
radiant with the goodness of life,
that has its source in you.

Through this sign of chrism
grant them royal, priestly, and prophetic honor,
and clothe them with incorruption.
Let this be indeed the chrism of salvation
for those who will be born again in water and the Holy Spirit.
May they come to share eternal life
in the glory of your kingdom. (25)

On Holy Saturday at the Easter Vigil, baptism in water is followed by anointing with chrism. The bishop (or presiding priest) prays over the newly baptized, saying:

The God of power and Father of our Lord Jesus Christ
has freed you from sin
and brought you to new life
through water and the Holy Spirit.

He now anoints you with the chrism of salvation,
so that, united with his people,
you may remain for ever a member of Christ
who is Priest, Prophet, and King. (228)

After the prayer the newly baptized are anointed on the crowns of their heads. The celebration continues with two explanatory rites: the clothing

with a baptismal garment and the presentation of a lighted candle. The
sacrament of confirmation follows for the newly baptized adults. Here
the presider evokes the sevenfold gifts of the Holy Spirit. With arms
stretched out over those to be confirmed, he prays:

> All-powerful God, Father of our Lord Jesus Christ,
> by water and the Holy Spirit
> you freed your sons and daughters from sin
> and gave them new life.
>
> Send your Holy spirit upon them
> to be their helper and guide.
>
> Give them the spirit of wisdom and understanding,
> the spirit of right judgment and courage,
> the spirit of knowledge and reverence.
> Fill them with the spirit of wonder and awe in your presence.
> We ask this through Christ our Lord. Amen. (234)

The presider then dips his thumb into the chrism and makes the sign of
the cross on the foreheads of the ones confirmed as he says, "Be sealed
with the gift of the Holy Spirit."

Although oil is the focus of the Chrism Mass as well as the medium of
sacramental anointings, the meaning of oil itself is obscured. The blessing
of oil and the prayers of anointing tell us little about the oil itself except
that it comes from olive trees. Beyond that, the only mention of the nature
of oil is that it makes things radiant. Oil's life-giving properties of healing, nutrition, warmth, and light are not included in these blessings and
prayers. This failure to reference the nature of olive oil, however, is not
surprising in light of the similarities between this prayer and that of the
Gelasian Sacramentary. In fact, this prayer, which has not been shortened
as the blessing of water has, differs only slightly from the Gelasian prayer.
The richness and flow of the ancient prayers are modernized, and yet,
sentence by sentence, the prayers repeat the same themes. The primary
difference in the prayers is that the conferral of the gifts of the Holy
Spirit is reserved for confirmation in the current prayer. This, however,
reflects a development in the administration of the sacraments rather
than a deepening awareness of the sacramental oil. Both prayers overlook
the nature of the olive oil used in the anointing rather than allowing it to
enrich the sacrament.

The connection between the physical properties and sacramental use of olive oil is at least partially retained in the *Catechism of the Catholic Church.* In the section on the "Celebration of the Christian Mystery," we read:

> Anointing, in biblical and other ancient symbolism, is rich in meaning: oil is a sign of abundance and joy, it cleanses (anointing before and after a bath) and limbers (the anointing of athletes and wrestlers); oil is a sign of healing, since it is soothing to bruises and wounds; and it makes radiant with beauty, health, and strength.
>
> Anointing with oil has all these meanings in the sacramental life. The pre-baptismal anointing with oil of catechumens signifies cleansing and strengthening; the anointing of the sick expresses healing and comfort. The post-baptismal anointing with sacred chrism in Confirmation and ordination is the sign of consecration. By Confirmation, Christians, that is, those who are anointed, share more completely in the mission of Jesus Christ and the fullness of the Holy Spirit with which he is filled, so that their lives may give off "the aroma of Christ."[38]

Although the authors of the *Catechism* were primarily drawing on biblical stories in this teaching, their mention of oil as a sign of abundance, health, strength, cleansing, and consecration resonates with the natural history of olive oil recounted earlier in the chapter. Even with this positive acknowledgment it is clear that many contemporary churches have lost the knowledge of the nature of olive oil. Traditionally, the sacred oils were stored in closed cupboards in the sanctuary of the church. However, it has become commonplace in newer churches to keep the oils beautifully illuminated in glass flasks in view of the congregation. Though such displays are intended to honor the sacramental, they betray a loss of knowledge about olive oil itself. With constant exposure to light and heat, olive oil spoils rapidly. Churches with these elegant displays risk baptizing their new members in rancid oil. What is needed is a deep knowledge of and intimacy with the oils themselves—not just their role in ritual, but also their very properties. Once such a relationship develops, liturgically-minded churches will once again veil their sacramental oil in ways that respect olive oil's joyful but demure nature.

38. CCC, 328.

From its beginning the tradition of anointing with oil was embedded in an olive culture where the nature of the oil needed no explication. In olive cultures the fecundity of olive trees ensured a generous annual yield of oil. Mediterranean people knew how to keep olive oil from spoiling, and so, unlike water, oil was easily available. In Mediterranean cultures, olives and olive oil were essential to so many aspects of daily life that they were easily taken for granted. Centuries after the anointing of Aaron, the Gelasian prayers also reveal the influence of olive culture. Because the prayers were written in Latin, which became the universal language of the church, there was no change in the prayers as Christianity spread around the globe and into cultures that did not share a Mediterranean use or knowledge of olive oil. The Latin prayers veiled Mediterranean assumptions about olive oil when they were brought into climates where olives did not flourish. The full significance of olive oil, understated and assumed in the Gelasian prayers, was all but lost in cultures that did not understand Latin. The significance of olive oil fared no better when the Latin prayers where translated into English for cultures that did not understand olives. An appreciation or tacit knowledge of the nature of olive oil cannot be assumed in climates that do not participate in olive culture. It is no wonder that the full sacramental significance of olive oil is lost and that in the most liturgically conscious churches it risks going rancid while it is beautifully displayed.

COSMOCENTRIC SACRAMENTALITY
AND OLIVE OIL

We have now traced the 13.7-billion-year story of olive oil. We began the story of oil at the birth of the Universe, when primary particles formed all the matter that would ever be. We saw those particles cluster into the stars that created all the elements that would eventually form oil in Earth's oceans. In this watery environment oil formed the membranes that enclosed and protected the first glimmers of life. We followed the story of living cells encased in oily membranes out of the oceans, into olives, and to the healthy shine on our faces. We then watched the shimmer of olive oil radiate from the stories of Aaron, the widows, and the temple, through bridesmaids and Jesus into the blessings and teaching of the church. In the cosmic story we saw oil as an essential constituent of all life. In the sacramental story this pervasiveness of olive oil continued as it made God's blessing visible with abundance and joy. In these stories the significance of oil, already shadowed by its own domesticity, slipped even farther from sight when the Mediterranean prayers spread into cultures where olives did not grow. Integrating the natural history and sacramental stories of olive oil has the potential to bring baptismal candidates into awareness of the generosity of God that has shone through oil since life began. Moreover, the integration of oil's stories becomes part of the foundation of a cosmocentric sacramentality.

As with water, the concept of thresholds developed by Pierre Teilhard de Chardin is helpful in the integration of the natural history and sacramental stories of oil. Recall that in this scheme Teilhard divided Earth's history into four phases: pre-life, life, thought, and superlife.[39] Oil's pre-life phase begins with the birth of the Universe and continues as oil forms lipid membranes in the oceans. Oil crosses the threshold into its life phase as membrane-embraced processes turn into living beings. Oil enters the thought phase as self-reflective consciousness emerges in humans. In this phase oil participates in the human adventure of development and self-knowledge. The superlife phase of oil emerges when self-aware humans begin to perceive themselves as part of the Earth community. This perception carries a nascent awareness of the reality of our planet into our consciousness. We belong to the life community of Earth. Our ability to perceive with each of our senses relies on the oil of our cellular membranes. Through the sensitivity we receive from oil we rejoice in the delicate beauty of Earth as never before, but simultaneously the suffering of Earth becomes unbearable. In the phase of superlife, as oil-rich beings we have the potential to celebrate the joys, to share the suffering, and to participate in the healing of the planet.

In summary, through these developmental stages the emphasis in the story of oil shifts from the inorganic to the living, to human thought, and finally to oil's planetary nature. In this final stage we experience ourselves not only in our particular human lineage, but also in oil's lineage, which stretches back 13.7 billion years to the Beginning and reaches ahead into the future. Teilhard's concept of thresholds in Earth's development places the person aware of this heritage within the unfolding cosmic and sacramental story of oil.

What might this awareness of oneself as participating in the radiance of oil mean to a person about to be anointed at baptism? In her cosmocentric

39. Pierre Teilhard de Chardin, *The Human Phenomenon*, trans. Sarah Appleton-Weber (Portland, OR: Sussex Academic Press, 2003).

reflection at least three insights might emerge. First, she would consider the appropriateness of using oil, especially olive oil, as the sacramental for making visible the invisible Spirit. As she ponders the history of oil she remembers that the first cellular membranes formed in the same way soap bubbles and ocean foam still do. She might smile as she thinks of these iridescent spheres and the joy that often attends them. She recalls also oil's plant history and stories of the first photosynthetic bacteria to capture sunlight. She puzzles over a whole kingdom of life forms that draw energy from the Sun and then feed it and themselves to the rest of the life-world. Self-sacrifice at the bottom of the food chain seems to be built into the plant world. She is cheered, however, by the ingenuity of flowering plants that learned to generously give away their sun-drenched nectar and fruit as a way to insure their own survival. Flowering plants' generosity fed their predators and perfected love of neighbor long before Jesus introduced the concept to humans.

Olive trees, she reflects, are particularly generous. Their fruit sustained foraging animals for thousands of years when winter foods were scarce. For the human communities where olive trees grew, olives and their oil became a staple of almost every aspect of life. Significantly, olive oil made things shine. Light, a symbol of God's presence, shimmered on everything touched by olive oil. Joy, generosity, and brilliance are all part of the history of olive oil, but there is one thing more that makes olive oil particularly suited to manifest the divine. In a pleasing irony she notices that the very oil that makes everything shine with God's pleasure, that makes visible the invisible Spirit, is often overlooked. She now knows that oil is as omnipresent in the Earth community as it was in the olive culture that birthed the Christian tradition, and even though it is often not seen or acknowledged, it remains as faithful as the widows in the books of Kings, or even, she might muse, as faithful as God. The generosity and joy of olive oil make it right for baptismal anointing.

As this person continues to reflect on herself as a participant in oil's radiance, a second insight might be that she already shares in the two anointings of which Irenaeus spoke. In the first anointing, the Word was anointed by God before the world began, and through the Word each being and thing was anointed as it was created. She might smile to think of oily membranes as anointing the first cells that came to life in the oceans. Perhaps the oily embrace of each cell, including those of her own body, somehow participates in that same primordial anointing. She might feel the oil that keeps her skin smooth and makes her face shine as the impress of that first anointing. Surprised by her joy, she slips into a level of intimacy with the powers of creation, more profound than she ever could have imagined.

In Irenaeus' second anointing she learned that Jesus was anointed at the Jordan and that his anointing radiated to every being and held the cosmos in a divine embrace. As a part of that cosmos she knows that she has received this second anointing as well. Already anointed twice over, what might she make of the anointing she is now about to receive? This baptismal anointing cannot be the moment when the Spirit rests upon her for the first time. Rather, she realizes that this third anointing is the celebration of the two universal anointings in her as a particular being. Her baptismal anointing makes visible and celebrates the unseen but eternally-present Spirit as it abides uniquely in her.

The third insight this radiant person might have concerns the sensitivity her oily membranes make possible. She remembers that it is her cell membranes, particularly the membranes of her nervous system, that allow her to feel and interpret the sensations she experiences. The sensitivity engendered in her over 13.7 billion years is not merely to feel pain, but to transmute it into an awareness of suffering. Even as her sensitivity and her growing awareness of the suffering of the Earth community draw her toward despair, she knows that anointing and oil are, nevertheless, about joy. She might recall the saying attributed to Pierre Teilhard de Chardin that "joy is the most infallible sign of the presence of God." She is reminded that Thomas Berry once said that the prophets Earth needs today must be able not only to take in the beauty of Earth, but also to look suffering in the face. As she ends her musing, she might recall the psalm that relates Aaron joyfully dripping with oil to the goodness of a close community and the return of the exiles. As her planetary consciousness deepens, she wonders whether humans, who have endured centuries of self-imposed exile, might finally be returning to the Earth community. She smiles as she thinks of the joy that home-coming would cause.

In Praise of Oil

> *Loving and Living God, we rejoice*
> *in your gift of Olive Oil for baptism,*
>
> *Oil that cradled nascent life in ancient oceans,*
> *Oil that embraces every cell of every being that ever lived*
> *Oil that stores the generosity of the Sun,*

Oil that glistened on Aaron's face and beard,
and whose miraculous abundance
    we celebrate at Chanukah.
Oil of widows and bridesmaids, radiant with fidelity,
Oil of anointing, presence of God made visible,
    hovering over the waters of creation,
        bearing the olive branch to Noah after the flood,
    appearing above the Jordan to announce
        Jesus as your beloved.
Oil of baptism that heals and seals us in your love.

Loving and living God, we rejoice
    in your gift of Olive Oil for baptism.

Chapter Three

FIRE

A Hymn to Fire

> Passionate, radiant God,
> Make us vibrant with your gift of fire in baptism.
>
> Fire born of stars and Earth,
> Life-air dance that stabilized the atmosphere,
> Burning within and not consuming,
> Illuminating, embracing energy, universal bond.
>
> Flame and light
> Warmth and caves
> Fire of torches, and candles, and lamps
> Lighting, heating, fighting, comforting
>
> Passion of God and Moses
> Burning bush and blazing pillar
> Sending, guiding
> Destroying enemies, accepting offerings and ourselves.
>
> Light of the world
> Stars, and Son, and us,
> Light in darkness and in day,
> Candles called to set the world ablaze.

Fire of God,
   Consume our offerings,
   Purify our love,
   Illumine the world.

Passionate, radiant God,
   Make us vibrant with your gift of fire in baptism.

Fire embraces the Universe. As flame, fire is an Earth-bound process. Yet as a source of light fire shares in the power and mystery of the Sun and stars, and even the light from the Beginning. In a process taking billions of years, the Sun shared its light-making ability with the maturing Earth. As the Sun continually bathed the Earth some bacteria developed the ability to absorb sunlight and then use it as energy. As a byproduct of photosynthesis, these bacteria released oxygen from water molecules into the ocean and atmosphere. Gradually the amount of oxygen in the ocean became dangerous to many creatures. Some two billion years after photosynthesis began, the planet was in peril. High levels of oxygen threatened to extinguish life on Earth. Life, however, is resilient. Initially some small beings adapted to the presence of oxygen and used it as fuel. Then larger beings engulfed these smaller ones and appropriated their success with oxygen for themselves. As they did, these beings developed respiration and Earth took its first breaths. Disaster was averted by single-celled creatures that converted a toxin to a fuel source and passed on that ability to all future generations of life.

Eventually, as the oxygen level increased, plants and then animals moved onto dry land. As plants spread across the continents their photosynthesis steadily increased the amount of oxygen in the air. Animal respiration removed only a small portion. When the oxygen level was high enough, lightning strikes that once merely smoldered now ignited and caused plants to burn. As the oxygen level continued to increase, fire spread across the continents, releasing stored sunlight in the form of flames.

Hundreds of millions of years later, one of Earth's creatures also appropriated the Sun's power to make light. As a consequence of human domestication of fire, the light of the Sun, which is impossible to look at directly, shines in the single flame of a candle that draws our gaze. Early humans never knew, and scientists only learned a few generations ago, that we also glow like candles. The same processes that cause a candle to burn enable respiration within our cells and the cells of all living beings.

The air we breathe and the food we eat mix in our cells and release energy. Like a candle flame, we radiate light every moment.

The light that radiates throughout the world shines in biblical stories from Genesis and the creation of the world to Revelation and the world's destruction. Fire in the Old Testament manifests God's presence, acceptance, and harsh judgment. In the New Testament fire as flame shows God's judgment, and as light it shines in Jesus and each of his followers. Fire—flame and light—shines in candles throughout the Christian tradition. Few Catholic liturgical celebrations occur without the presence of candlelight.

Like the blessings that begin the two previous chapters, this hymn to fire weaves both the scientific and the sacred stories into a hymn of praise. Through this integration the prayer acknowledges the physical as well as the symbolic importance of fire in salvation history.

THE NATURAL HISTORY OF FIRE

The blaze of wildfires and the warm glow of candles exist only on Earth. There is no evidence that fuel and oxygen, the two things required for fire, exist together anywhere in the Solar System or any place in the Universe other than on Earth. Although there may be something to provide fuel on other planets, such as methane on Venus, only Earth is known to have the concentration of oxygen required for fire.[1] Our Sun and stars certainly glow with fire-like brilliance, but their light and heat come from nuclear fusion, not fire. The fire that lit our ancestors' dark nights and warms us still is an Earth-born energy.

Wild Fire

> *Passionate, radiant God,*
> > *Make us vibrant with your gift of fire in baptism.*
> *Fire born of stars and Earth,*
> > *Life-air dance that stabilized the atmosphere,*
> > *Burning within and not consuming,*
> > *Illuminating, embracing energy, universal bond.*

1. For a description of the composition of celestial bodies in our Solar System see Roger A. Freedman and William J. Kaufmann, *Universe*, 6th ed. (New York: W. H. Freeman, 2002).

The elements that compose all things on Earth have their origins in the Beginning. As we saw in the story of water, hydrogen formed within the first fractions of a second of the Universe's life. Some of this hydrogen clustered and collapsed together to form stars. Certain stars were large enough to fuse hydrogen and helium into carbon and oxygen and all the other elements. When the primordial stars died they released their elements into interstellar space. The elements mixed in space, forming water and other compounds. Later, during the formation of the Solar System, these elements and compounds gathered to form Earth, its oceans, and eventually, life.

Fire became a possibility on Earth when light-sensitive beings began to exhale oxygen. Cyanobacteria developed photosynthesis 3.8 billion years ago and started the release of oxygen from ocean water into the atmosphere. One billion years ago, sufficient exhaled oxygen had bubbled into the atmosphere to create a protective blanket of ozone that allowed bacteria to move onto dry land without being destroyed by ultraviolet radiation. Four hundred and twenty-five million years ago, as the ozone layer thickened and when the oxygen levels in the atmosphere reached just two percent, algae were able to survive on dry land.[2] With the spread of plants across the continents, Earth was covered with photosynthetic beings and the amount of atmospheric oxygen increased rapidly.

Through the Carboniferous and Permian periods (360 to 251 million years ago), atmospheric oxygen levels fluctuated between 15 and 35 percent. Below 15 percent fire is not possible; above 25 percent even wet organic material burns easily. As forests stretched across the continents, plants released large amounts of oxygen, raising the oxygen level in the atmosphere and the probability of fire. Sparked by lightning or volcanism, fires raged. They consumed the oxygen-producing forests, which in turn diminished the possibility of fire, and simultaneously created a blanket of ash that fertilized the next generation of trees. This cycle continued for millions of years. Eventually the fluctuations in oxygen levels, driven by alternating periods of vast fires and rapid plant growth, began to stabilize.

Plants made fire possible by releasing oxygen into the atmosphere and by offering themselves as fuel. Their cycles of burning and photosynthesizing balanced oxygen at a level that allowed for the further flowering of Earth. Since the beginning of the Mesozoic era, 250 million years ago, the oxygen level in the atmosphere has remained at a precarious 21 percent.

2. Thomas L. Rost, Michael G. Barbour, C. Ralph Stocking, and Terence M. Murphy, *Plant Biology* (Davis, CA: Wadsworth, 1998), 385.

If it were lower, animals as we know them would not have enough oxygen to breathe. If it were higher, life would be destroyed in flames. As we saw in the chapter on oil, once again plants established the conditions for life to flourish on Earth.

Domestic Fire

> *Passionate, radiant God,*
> > *Make us vibrant with your gift of fire in baptism.*
> *Flame and light,*
> > *Warmth and caves,*
> > *Fire of torches, and candles, and lamps,*
> > *Lighting, heating, fighting, comforting.*

Hominids first deepened their friendship with fire some one million years ago. Ancient fire sites in Kenya and South Africa suggest that *Homo erectus* may have been our first ancestor to use fire. Long before they developed ways to ignite fire themselves, evidence suggests that early people watched for wildfires and then learned to tend them. They sought out naturally occurring fires, kept them burning, and carried pieces of this fire in the form of burning branches or coals to shelters and tended them there. Fire was used for warmth, lighting, cooking, defense, and hunting. In hunting it was used to harden wood and flint, drive prey, and burn brush for increased visibility. As knowledge of fire grew, people noticed that better grassland grew after a fire and that better grasses led to more plentiful game. Although *Homo erectus* used fire, evidence that they made fire has not been uncovered.[3]

Hundreds of thousands of years later, intimacy with fire deepened as *Homo sapiens* found ways to kindle their own fire. The same skills used for working stone and bone developed into methods for igniting flames. Fire-making tools included friction tools such as drills and saws, and stones that created sparks such as flints and pyrites. The first indications of fire starters are deeply grooved balls of iron pyrite found in Neolithic villages that thrived fifteen thousand years ago.[4] In these early settlements fire assisted in the advent of agriculture. It was used to clear land for planting and to remove stubble after the fields were harvested. The ash produced

3. John Relethford, *The Human Species: An Introduction to Biological Anthropology,* 5th ed. (New York: McGraw Hill, 2003), 376.
4. Ibid.

by burning fertilized the fields. As their intimacy with fire deepened, *Homo sapiens* extended the use of fire to pottery making and metallurgy.

Toward Candles

Within the history of fire the story of candles begins with torches. It is likely that burning branches pulled from a fire were the first torches to provide portable light.[5] Modifications in torches led to candles. In one modification bundled branches were coated with flammable substances such as resin, pitch, or wax.[6] In another variation branches were replaced with twisted rope coated in flammable materials. In another innovation the use of splinters of wood or rushes (a type of reed) decreased the size of torches, making them easy to carry. Splinters were narrow strips of resinous wood such as pine that were cut to uniform lengths and dried. They were held at an angle and lit at the lower end so that the flame would burn up the stick, providing light. Rushlights were splinters of various woods or rushes that were soaked in water, dried, and dipped in flammable materials such as animal fats. These were burnt at an angle and lit at the top end, which allowed the tallow to run down the stick. Candles were similar to these in that they shared the principle of a wick coated with a waxy substance. Candles, however, had a thicker coating, a longer life, and were burnt upright.[7]

Although the manufacture of candles improved, olive oil lamps became common around the Mediterranean. The use of candles, however, was maintained in ritual celebrations.[8] As the Roman Empire spread north into the forests of Europe and away from olive cultivation, the extensive use of candles followed. Candles remained a common source of light in early medieval Europe and predominated in cooler climates far from supplies of Mediterranean olive oil.

Candles

The first modern candles, developed by the Romans, were papyrus wicks dipped in tallow or beeswax.[9] Tallow candles, which were made

---

5. F. W. Robins, *The Story of the Lamp (and the Candle)* (New York: Oxford University Press, 1939), 6.

6. Ibid., 7.

7. *Early Lighting: A Pictorial Guide* (Hartford, CT: The Rushlight Club, 1972), 17.

8. Robins, *The Story of the Lamp (and the Candle)*, 8.

9. Ibid., 16.

from rendered animal fat, were smoky, drippy, and odorous. Beeswax candles burned more cleanly, but they were costly. Until the fifteenth century their use was limited almost exclusively to church ceremonies.[10] Candle-making guilds formed by the thirteenth century. Examples in London include the Worshipful Company of Waxchandlers, which dates to 1358, and the Tallowchandlers, which was chartered in 1462.[11]

The next great innovation in candle making occurred in eighteenth-century Europe when an efficient means was developed for killing sperm whales. An adult sperm whale has a wagon-sized cavity in its head used for hearing; it is full of a crystalline substance called spermaceti. Refined spermaceti became widely used for candles, displacing tallow and beeswax. Spermaceti candles could be cast in molds rather than being dipped, making their manufacture less time-consuming. Spermaceti candles became the standard for the measurement of artificial light. One candlepower was the measurement of light given off by a pure spermaceti candle weighing one-sixth of a pound and burning at 120 grains per hour.[12]

Other developments in candle making soon followed. In the early 1800s wicks of braided cotton replaced wicks of flax and twisted fibers. These naturally-bending cotton wicks were self-snuffing. The tip of the wick bent through the flame, where it was exposed to air and burned off, thus diminishing the need to be trimmed.[13] In another development, in 1823, stearine, the white portion of animal fat, was separated out of the fats used for tallow. Stearine produced a cleaner-burning and less odorous candle. This advantage was little used, however, because in 1850 paraffin wax, a purified petroleum product, began to be used for candles. Paraffin candles gave off a brighter light and, like spermaceti candles, could be made in molds instead of by dipping. By the end of the nineteenth century clean, bright paraffin candles were displaced by electric lights as the primary light source in Europe.[14]

Candle Flame

Now that we have traced the emergence of fire on Earth and then followed its human domestication from flaming branches to paraffin candles,

10. Ibid., 17.
11. Ibid., 18.
12. Ibid., 20. A grain is a measure of weight equal to 1/7000 pound or 64.8 milligrams; 120 grains equal 7.77 grams.
13. *Early Lighting: A Pictorial Guide*, 17.
14. Robins, *The Story of the Lamp (and the Candle)*, 20.

we focus our gaze on the twin aspects of fire, its flame and its light. To understand fire's flame we investigate combustion, and to better know fire's light we explore electromagnetism.

Combustion

Fuel, oxygen, and a spark are required to light a fire. In the case of a candle, the spark is generally supplied by striking a match. Once the candle is lit, the wick itself provides the initial fuel, and the surrounding air supplies the oxygen. The heat from the burning wick quickly begins to melt the candle below, forming a cup of liquid wax. The wax in the cup first wets the base of the wick and is then absorbed up the wick. As a wax particle reaches the flame, it burns and is followed by another particle.[15]

The flame of a candle has two areas that, when the flame is reasonably still, resemble nested cones. The darker, often blue, inner cone consists of wax particles that have been turned to vapor by the heat of the flame. The outer, often orange cone is the combustion zone—the area where the hot vapor mixes with the oxygen in the air. The bright line where these cones meet is made of wax vapor superheated into plasma.[16] The wick of most candles curves through the inner cone to the edge of the combustion zone, where its tip glows as it burns.

Combustion in a candle is the reaction between wax vapor, which is made primarily of hydrocarbons (molecules composed of hydrogen and carbon atoms) and oxygen in the air. As particles of wax move up the wick and become increasingly hot they are changed from a liquid to a vapor. This vapor moves away from the wick and is mixed with the oxygen in the air in the combustion zone. Where the vapor and the oxygen first meet, the heat generated is great enough to transform the vapor into plasma by cracking the hydrocarbons into hydrogen and carbon nuclei.[17] Oxygen mixes with the hydrogen to form water vapor and with the carbon to form

15. Michael Faraday, *The Chemical History of a Candle* (New York: Dover Publications, 2002).

16. Plasma is the fourth state of matter and is distinct from solid, liquid, and gas. On Earth plasma occurs naturally only in flames. It also exists in stars and was the material state of the Universe for the 380,000 years before atoms formed.

17. N. R. Mukherjee, "Flames," *Encyclopaedic Dictionary of Physics: General, Nuclear, Solid State, Molecular Chemical, Metal and Vacuum Physics, Astronomy, Geophysics, Biophysics, and Related Subjects*, ed. James Thewlis, et al. (New York: Pergamon Press, 1961), 164–68.

carbon dioxide.[18] Some of the particles in the wax plasma are not burned completely. These particles glow in the heat of the flame and release electromagnetic radiation, which gives the flame its luminosity. As they release light these unburned particles are carried out of the flame by air currents and leave as soot. Through combustion a candle is transformed into water, carbon dioxide, a little soot, and light.

Electromagnetism

Electromagnetism is one of the four fundamental interactions that describe all the relationships between matter and energy in the Universe.[19] This interaction describes how light is radiated and how matter is held together at the atomic and molecular levels. When the wax of a candle melts in the heat of a flame, it changes from a solid to a liquid state. The wax is further heated as it moves up the wick and closer to the flame, where it changes states again, is vaporized, and then is transformed into plasma. In this process heat excites the atoms in the wax, which causes some of their electrons to jump to higher energy levels and breaks some of the bonds that hold the atoms together. Photons (particles of light) released by this change in energy level and the breaking of atomic bonds cause the flame to glow.

Reciprocally, when the candle is cool the electromagnetic interaction holds the atomic structure of the wax together. Electromagnetism is the force that bonds charged particles of matter. It forms atoms by bonding positively charged atomic nuclei to negatively charged electrons. It also forms molecules by bonding atoms together. Energy is trapped in atoms and molecules held together by electromagnetism and released in the form of photons when the bonds break. The electromagnetic bonds in atoms and molecules are continually shifting. Each time a photon is absorbed, another is released. Most of the photons released are quickly absorbed by other atoms. This dance of release and absorption continues in all matter. Of the trillions of light particles released every second by the objects around us, only a small portion is visible to us as light and color. Photons released by matter radiate across the spectrum from ultraviolet to infrared

18. Faraday, *The Chemical History of a Candle*, 68. According to Faraday, as a pint of oil burns it creates more than a pint of water.

19. The four fundamental interactions are: electromagnetism, gravity, the strong nuclear, and the weak nuclear. For a description of the four fundamental interactions see especially chap. 29 in Freedman and Kaufmann, *Universe*.

and microwaves. Without mechanical assistance, humans only perceive a small portion of the light in which we are constantly bathed.

Fire in Our Own Bodies

The two aspects of candle flame seen above, combustion and electromagnetism, also appear in our own bodies. The process of combustion in a candle is remarkably similar to the process of respiration in our cells. The electromagnetic interaction not only holds all the atoms and molecules of our cells together but also causes them to emit photons of light.

Respiration

Michael Faraday (1791–1867), a British physicist legendary for his contributions to the study of electromagnetism, describes how human respiration and a candle's combustion use the same process. In an annual series of Christmas lectures called "The Chemical History of a Candle," he excitedly told his students: "Now I must take you to a very interesting part of our subject—to the relationship between the combustion of a candle and that living kind of combustion, which goes on within us. In every one of us, there is a living process of combustion going on very similar to that of a candle, and I must try to make that plain to you. For it is not merely true in a poetical sense—the relation of the life of [a person] to a taper."[20]

Faraday compares the combustion of a candle to respiration in a person, explaining that both mix oxygen from the air with fuel. The candle flame uses molten wax drawn up a wick; the lungs use dissolved nutrients carried in the blood. In the lungs, oxygen and hydrocarbons from the blood supply mix across a thin membrane and then release carbon dioxide, water, and heat.[21] The oxidation in a candle flame is rapid and luminous while the same process in the human is slow and less visible, yet in fact it is the identical process.

Faraday may not have been aware that the same process he understood as happening in candles and our lungs also happens in the cells of every living being. In mammals such as ourselves the oxygen in the air we inhale diffuses across membranes in our lungs. As the oxygen-rich blood pulses through our tiny capillaries it diffuses across membranes into oxygen-

20. Faraday, *The Chemical History of a Candle*, 167.
21. Ibid., 174–76.

depleted cells. Once it reaches the watery interior of a cell, the oxygen is picked up by mitochondria, the tiny lungs in all living cells.

There are ten to twenty thousand mitochondria in a single cell, depending on a particular cell's function. In each mitochondrion oxygen mixes with nutrients, which generates energy for the cell and for the body. In the process the mitochondria burn carbon and release carbon dioxide and water. Blood picks up these byproducts of cellular respiration and carries them to the lungs, where they are released from our bodies in exhalation. Like the combustion of a candle flame, the respiration of our bodies burns carbon in oxygen and releases water and carbon dioxide. Moreover, like a candle flame, these cells also release light.

Humans and other mammals are not the only beings that glow with respiration. All beings with nucleated cells have mitochondria, which oxidize sugars and release energy. Even plants respire. The sugars they produce through photosynthesis are later oxidized to provide energy for the plant. Not only humans, but all living beings share in the same luminous process as the flame of a candle.

Electromagnetism

One of the four primary interactions used to describe the behavior of matter and energy, electromagnetism is the interaction that attracts electrons to atomic nuclei and forms atoms into molecules. *Every atom and molecule in our bodies, and in everything else*, is held together by the electromagnetic interaction. If it were interrupted for even a fraction of a second, everything would dissipate into plasma. The electromagnetic interaction holds everything together on a microcosmic level.

In addition to its attractive properties, electromagnetism is also responsible for light. In fact, electromagnetic radiation is light. Everything above absolute zero, the temperature at which all atomic activity stops, emits light. Electrons are never still. As they flash around their atomic centers, they absorb and release energy. When a particle of light, or photon, hits an atom, two things can happen. Either the photon bounces off the atom and we see it as glare, or it is absorbed by the atom. When the atom absorbs a photon, it becomes excited and then emits another photon, which we see as color. This photon we see as color is not the same photon that hit the atom; that one melted into the atom. This new particle was created by the atom itself. The particles of light we see as color do not simply bounce off the things around us; the things around us create them.

Every atom of every thing, including the trillions of atoms in our skin, is constantly interacting with photons and emitting light. Only a small portion of the light ever reaches perceiving eyes, and a still smaller portion of that light is in the spectrum visible to humans. Nevertheless, the light released by our skin and the clothes we wear is absorbed into the people and material around us. Reciprocally, our bodies absorb light emanated from all the objects and bodies around us at all times. When a child sees his father's smile, the light emitted from his father reaches the child's eyes and then his sensitive nerve cells interpret the image. However, the light emitted by the atoms of his father's face is not limited to those that meet his eyes; his entire body absorbs light from his father and from everything else in the room. Like the father and the child, each of us is broadcasting light in every direction at every moment. Everything is constantly shining light toward everything else.[22] We are pillars of light.

THE SACRAMENTAL STORY OF FIRE

The fire that embraces the Universe also radiates through the celebration of baptism. The sacramental story of fire begins with Old Testament accounts in which fire plays a central part and continues with narratives from the New Testament. After recalling the most significant biblical sources of fire that lead to its use in baptism we view ancient and contemporary practices of the church in respect to fire. As a means of tracing the lineage of the lit candle of baptism we consider the paschal candle and blessings of fire used in the Easter Vigil.

Fire's Biblical Source

Old Testament
> Passionate, radiant God,
> > Make us vibrant with your gift of fire in baptism.
> Passion of God and Moses,
> > Burning bush and blazing pillar,
> > Sending, guiding,
> > Destroying enemies, accepting offerings, and ourselves.

22. Because it travels at a constant velocity, the light released by a four-year-old at his birth has already traveled twenty-five trillion miles, or four light years, and has just reached Proxima Centauri, our nearest star other than the sun. The light emitted when his father was born some twenty-five years earlier is just reaching Vega, one of the brightest stars in the northern summer sky.

In the Old Testament fire is multivalent.[23] It is used for cooking, manu-
facturing, metalwork, and as a weapon of war. On the sabbath kindling
fires is prohibited, but altar fires used for sacrificial purposes are tended
with reverence. Images of fire are used to symbolize destructive human
passions such as rage, and to describe forces that cannot be resisted, such
as forest fires, refining ovens, and lightning. God is fiery. In theophanies
such as the one experienced by Moses at the burning bush and Ezekiel's
vision of divine radiance, fire reveals God's holiness and glory. God's
grace is manifest as fire that accepts sacrifices, provides protection and
guidance, and receives Elijah in a fiery chariot. Time and again in the
Old Testament, God appears as an all-consuming fire, a majestic being
of grace and judgment.

The Burning Bush

Genesis recounts how drought brought the nomadic Hebrews to the
land of Egypt, where they became slaves. Eventually Pharaoh becomes
so afraid of their burgeoning numbers that he orders the midwives to kill
all the newborn Hebrew boys as soon as they enter the world. Through
a conspiracy of women the baby Moses is saved from death and raised in
the household of the Pharaoh.[24] As he grows, Moses cannot reconcile his
position of privilege with the Hebrews' life of oppression. In a fit of rage
he kills an Egyptian taskmaster and flees to the desert where he marries
and becomes a shepherd. One day, while tending a flock on Mount Horeb
(also called Sinai), Moses is attracted to a sight that kindles his passion
and eventually frees the Hebrews from slavery.

> Moses was keeping the flock of his father-in-law Jethro, the priest of
> Midian; he led his flock beyond the wilderness, and came to Horeb, the
> mountain of God. There the angel of the LORD appeared to him in a flame
> of fire out of a bush; he looked, and the bush was blazing, yet it was not

23. For an extensive treatment of fire in the Old and New Testaments see Friedrich
Lang, art. πῦρ, κτλ., in Gerhard Kittel, Geoffrey William Bromiley, and Gerhard
Friedrich, *Theological Dictionary of the New Testament* (Grand Rapids: Eerdmans,
1964), 6:928–52.

24. In this conspiracy the Egyptian midwives disobey Pharaoh and allow Moses to
be delivered safely. Moses' mother puts him in a basket in the river and sends Moses'
sister to look after him. The Pharaoh's daughter finds the baby and instantly decides
to keep him. Just as she is wondering about a wet nurse for the infant, Moses' sister
appears and offers to take him to her mother. She returns Moses to their mother and,
after he is weaned, Moses is sent back to the daughter of Pharaoh.

consumed. Then Moses said, "I must turn aside and look at this great sight, and see why the bush is not burned up." When the LORD saw that he had turned aside to see, God called to him out of the bush, "Moses, Moses!" And he said, "Here I am." Then he said, "Come no closer! Remove the sandals from your feet, for the place on which you are standing is holy ground." He said further, "I am the God of your father, the God of Abraham, the God of Isaac, and the God of Jacob." And Moses hid his face, for he was afraid to look at God.

Then the LORD said, "I have observed the misery of my people who are in Egypt; I have heard their cry on account of their taskmasters. Indeed, I know their sufferings, and I have come down to deliver them from the Egyptians . . . . The cry of the Israelites has now come to me; I have also seen how the Egyptians oppress them. So come, I will send you to Pharaoh to bring my people, the Israelites, out of Egypt." But Moses said to God, "Who am I that I should go to Pharaoh, and bring the Israelites out of Egypt?" He said, "I will be with you; and this shall be the sign for you that it is I who sent you: when you have brought the people out of Egypt, you shall worship God on this mountain." (Exodus 3:1-7, 9-13)

The conversation between God, speaking through the burning bush, and Moses continues for several verses as Moses tries to refuse God's proposal. After many excuses and much convincing, Moses accepts the responsibility to return to Egypt to liberate his people. Initially drawn by curiosity, in the presence of fire Moses comes to understand himself as empowered by God for this task. The burning bush reveals God to Moses and then reveals Moses to himself. In this story God is shown as fire that burns but does not consume. God is a blaze that attracts, commands, argues, and relents. God is a fire who has compassion for the suffering Hebrews. Moses' passion once forced him to leave Egypt. Now, with a fire burning within him, he returns.

The Pillar of Fire

In our second story of fire in the Old Testament, the Pillar of Fire, Moses has succeeded in bringing the Israelites out of Egypt. Pharaoh, worn down by plagues and grieved by the death of his son, releases the Hebrew people. Moses and a pillar of fire lead them from Egypt into the desert.

They set out from Succoth, and camped at Etham, on the edge of the wilderness. The LORD went in front of them in a pillar of cloud by day, to lead them along the way, and in a pillar of fire by night, to give them light, so that they might travel by day and by night. Neither the pillar of cloud by day nor the pillar of fire by night left its place in front of the people. (Exodus 13:20-22)

The pillar of fire not only leads the Israelites and stays with them; it also fights for them as they escape across the Red Sea. Pharaoh changes his mind and sends his army to capture the fleeing slaves. As the Egyptians close in on the Hebrews the pillar of fire leaves the front of the Hebrew camp to hold back the approaching army. All that night the fire casts a shadow on the Egyptians and light on the Israelites while Moses and a strong east wind drive back the waters of the Red Sea. After the Israelites are safely across the sea, "the LORD in the pillar of fire and cloud looked down upon the Egyptian army, and threw the Egyptian army into panic" and they perish in the sea (Exod 14:24). The presence of God in the form of cloud and fire remains constantly with the people as they sojourn in the desert for the next forty years. God as fire and cloud is the determination that drives, guides, comforts, and assures the people. In this story fire shows God's fierce care and abiding presence.

Solomon's Dedication of the Temple

By the time of our third story, Solomon's Dedication of the Temple, generations have passed since the Israelites crossed into the Promised Land. Israel is now a kingdom and Solomon its third king. Jerusalem is a thriving city as King Solomon completes the construction of a temple for the Lord. In the ceremony of dedication the ark of the covenant is joyously placed in the center of the temple and Solomon offers a lengthy prayer asking God to be attentive to prayers offered there.

> When Solomon had ended his prayer, fire came down from heaven and consumed the burnt offering and the sacrifices; and the glory of the LORD filled the temple. The priests could not enter the house of the LORD, because the glory of the LORD filled the LORD's house. When all the people of Israel saw the fire come down and the glory of the LORD on the temple, they bowed down on the pavement with their faces to the ground, and worshiped and gave thanks to the LORD, saying,
> "For he is good,
> for his steadfast love endures forever." (2 Chronicles 7:1-3)

In this story fire manifests God through its power to burn and to radiate light. The fire that fills the temple recalls the fire of the burning bush and the pillar that accompanied the pilgrim nation of Israel. God's glory shines as fire, consumes the offerings of the people, and fills the temple with unapproachable light.

Elijah on Mount Carmel

By the time of the stories of Elijah in the books of Kings, several dynasties of unfaithful kings have ruled Israel. The kings had become progressively worse, and God's anger was roused. The story of Elijah on Mount Carmel begins with King Ahab, who worships Baal while his wife Jezebel, the daughter of a pagan king, persecutes the prophets of God. In this dangerous situation Elijah, the chief prophet, predicts a drought that will only abate at his word. After he has made his pronouncement, God tells Elijah to flee to a stream across the Jordan where he will find sufficient water. Even this water eventually dries up, and God tells Elijah to go to Zarephath, where he helps a widow by multiplying her meal and oil.[25] In the third year of the drought God sends Elijah back to King Ahab. Once there, Elijah orders the king to assemble the Israelites as well as the four hundred fifty prophets of Baal and the four hundred prophets of Asherah on Mount Carmel. In the midst of the crowd, Elijah asks the people to choose between the Lord and Baal, saying, "If the LORD is God, follow him; but if Baal, then follow him" (1 Kgs 18:21). The people do not answer, so Elijah offers a challenge: "Let two bulls be given to us; let [the prophets of Baal] choose one bull for themselves, cut it in pieces, and lay it on the wood, but put no fire to it; I will prepare the other bull and lay it on the wood, but put no fire to it. Then you call on the name of your god and I will call on the name of the LORD; the god who answers by fire is indeed God (1 Kgs 18:23-24)."

The prophets of Baal accept the challenge and prepare their bull, but from morning to noon, cry as they might to Baal, no fire comes. Elijah mocks the prophets of Baal and then calls the Israelites:

> "Come closer to me"; and all the people came closer to him. First he repaired the altar of the LORD that had been thrown down . . . . with the stones he built an altar in the name of the LORD. Then he made a trench around the altar, large enough to contain two measures of seed. Next he put the wood in order, cut the bull in pieces, and laid it on the wood. He said, "Fill four jars with water and pour it on the burnt offering and on the wood." Then he said, "Do it a second time"; and they did it a second time. Again he said, "Do it a third time"; and they did it a third

---

25. See chap. 2, pp. 50–51, "Elisha and the Widow's Oil."

time, so that the water ran all around the altar, and filled the trench also with water.

At the time of the offering of the oblation, the prophet Elijah came near and said, "O LORD, God of Abraham, Isaac, and Israel, let it be known this day that you are God in Israel, that I am your servant, and that I have done all these things at your bidding. Answer me, O LORD, answer me, so that this people may know that you, O LORD, are God, and that you have turned their hearts back." Then the fire of the LORD fell and consumed the burnt offering, the wood, the stones, and the dust, and even licked up the water that was in the trench. When all the people saw it, they fell on their faces and said, "The LORD indeed is God; the LORD indeed is God." (1 Kgs 18:30, 32-39)

Elijah then orders the people to gather the false prophets together and slaughter them in the Kidron Valley. Alone again, Elijah prays seven times for God to end the drought. As the rains begin to fall, he flees to Mount Horeb to avoid the wrath of Jezebel.

In this story fire is proof that Elijah's Lord is indeed the one God. In a fiery theophany God descends on Elijah's offering and consumes every bit of it, even the water that fills the trough. Fire's lack of response to the prophets of Baal brings condemnation on them. Fire here is taken as the sure sign of God's presence. Moreover, the fiery response to Elijah's challenge and prayer marks Elijah as a true prophet whose works coincide with the will of God.

New Testament

> *Passionate, radiant God,*
> > *Make us vibrant with your gift of fire in baptism.*
> *Light of the world,*
> > *Stars, and Son, and us,*
> > *Light in darkness and in day,*
> > *Candles called to set the world ablaze.*

In the New Testament fire no longer manifests God as the passionate force that consumes sacrifices, overwhelms temples, and fights battles. Rather, in the New Testament fire is the light that the incarnate Word brings into the world. As we shall see, this divine passion no longer resides with the First Person of the Trinity alone, but with Jesus and his followers. Stories of fire in the New Testament include allusions to hell and everlasting punishment as well as apocalyptic visions of Christ coming as a fiery avenger. There are mandates to keep lamps lit and to shine in the darkness, and there is Peter's firelit denial and later reconciliation. Of all the stories that tell us of fire and God, four narratives—baptism with fire and the Holy Spirit, the transfiguration, the light of the world, and Pentecost—lead most directly to the presentation of a lighted candle in baptism.

Baptism with the Holy Spirit and Fire

In this story John the Baptist is preaching at the Jordan River. He admonishes the people who come to him to repent of their sins and be baptized. When John sees a group of religious leaders coming for baptism, his tone harshens. "You brood of vipers!" he rages, "Who warned you to flee from the wrath to come?" (Matt 3:7). John continues: "I baptize you with water for repentance, but one who is more powerful than I is coming after me; I am not worthy to carry his sandals. He will baptize you with the Holy Spirit and fire. His winnowing fork is in his hand, and he will clear his threshing floor and will gather his wheat into the granary; but the chaff he will burn with unquenchable fire" (Matt 3:11-12).

Fire here is not something that accepts the offering of a devoted prophet. Rather, like the fire that destroyed the enemies of the Israelites, the baptism of fire destroys those whom God judges unworthy. The baptism John offers is one of repentance that prepares for the coming kingdom. John preaches that soon the time to repent will be over. When the messiah comes, he will baptize with fire and eternal judgment.

The Transfiguration

Our second story, the Transfiguration, is placed in Matthew's gospel after Jesus asks his disciples, "Who do you say that I am?"—to which Peter responds to Jesus that he is the Christ. Subsequent to Peter's profession, Jesus foretells his own death and teaches about the conditions of following him. Six days later

> Jesus took with him Peter and James and his brother John and led them up a high mountain, by themselves. And he was transfigured before them, and his face shone like the sun, and his clothes became dazzling white. Suddenly there appeared to them Moses and Elijah, talking with him. Then Peter said to Jesus, "Lord, it is good for us to be here; if you wish, I will make three dwellings here, one for you, one for Moses, and one for Elijah." While he was still speaking, suddenly a bright cloud overshadowed them, and from the cloud a voice said, "This is my Son, the Beloved; with him I am well pleased; listen to him!" When the disciples heard this, they fell to the ground and were overcome by fear. But

Jesus came and touched them, saying, "Get up and do not be afraid."
And when they looked up, they saw no one except Jesus himself alone.
(Matthew 17:1-8)

Jesus' transfiguration on a mountaintop is reminiscent of Moses and
the burning bush of Mount Sinai and Elijah and the fire of Mount Carmel.
Both of these Old Testament prophets associated with fire appear now
with Jesus as he shines like the Sun and becomes as dazzling as light.
When Solomon prayed that God would listen to prayers uttered at the
temple, the glory of God filled the temple with an unbearable light that
caused the frightened priests to flee. Jesus' radiance and the voice from
the bright cloud frighten the three apostles but do not drive them away;
rather, their fear is calmed. The transfiguration of Jesus reveals him as
more than a prophet like Moses and Elijah; he is the very light of God.
Like the light that filled the temple with God's glory, Jesus is the light
of God that fills the world.

The Light of the World
In the New Testament we read that God is light, that Jesus is the
light of the world, and then that *we* are the light of the world. In the first
letter of John we read: "We are writing these things so that our joy may
be complete. This is the message we have heard from him and proclaim
to you, that God is light and in him there is no darkness at all" (1 John
1:4-5). Connecting the light of God to Jesus, we read in the prologue of
John's gospel:

> In the beginning was the Word, and the Word was with God, and the Word
> was God. He was in the beginning with God. All things came into being
> through him, and without him not one thing came into being. What has
> come into being in him was life, and the life was the light of all people.
> The light shines in the darkness, and the darkness did not overcome
> it. . . . The true light, which enlightens everyone, was coming in to the
> world. (John 1:1-5, 9)

Later in John's gospel Jesus speaks of himself, saying, "I am the light of the
world. Whoever follows me will never walk in darkness but will have the
light of life" (John 8:12). Additional references to Jesus as the light of the
world are found at the beginning and end of his life. In Matthew's gospel
the star of Bethlehem leads the magi from the east to Jesus' cradle (Matt
2:1). In Luke's gospel the glory of God shines on the shepherds and sends
them to Bethlehem (Luke 2:8-20). At the end of Jesus' life Luke tells

us, "darkness came over the whole land until three in the afternoon" and at the moment of Jesus' death, "the sun's light failed" (Luke 23:44-45). Similarly, we read in Matthew and Mark: "From noon on [Mark: when it was noon] darkness came over the whole land until three in the afternoon (Matt 27:45; Mark 15:33).

Light comes into the world with Jesus' birth and falters with his death. These verses reveal Jesus to be the same light as the glory of God that filled the temple and the pillar of fire that guided the Israelites to freedom, as well as the source of light and life for all creation.

God is light. Jesus is light, and his followers shine with light. In Matthew's gospel, soon after Jesus calls his disciples, he preaches the Sermon on the Mount, telling those gathered around him: "You are the light of the world. A city built on a hill cannot be hid. No one after lighting a lamp puts it under the bushel basket, but on the lampstand, and it gives light to all in the house. In the same way, let your light shine before others, so that they may see your good works and give glory to your Father in heaven (Matt 5:14-16). In this proclamation we learn that each disciple of Jesus is called to shine with the presence of God. Jesus brings God's fiery presence into the world and becomes the light that illumines everyone.

Pentecost

Our final story leading to the use of lighted candles in baptism occurs at Pentecost. Fifty days after Passover the Jews celebrate the theophany of Sinai, the place where God gave Moses the Ten Commandments, and where Moses encountered God through the burning bush. On this day of celebration we find a group of Jesus' disciples meeting in a closed room.

> When the day of Pentecost had come, they were all together in one place. And suddenly from heaven there came a sound like the rush of a violent wind, and it filled the entire house where they were sitting. Divided tongues, as of fire, appeared among them, and a tongue rested on each of them. All of them were filled with the Holy Spirit and began to speak in other languages, as the Spirit gave them ability. (Acts 2:1-4)

The author's use of the image of tongues of flames to portray the descent of the Spirit recalls Moses' conversation with God in the burning bush. On Sinai the burning bush started the adventure of Moses and the Hebrew people. At Pentecost tongues of fire burn not in one place, speaking to one person, but in all the disciples, speaking to people of many languages. The fire that mediated God's words in the Old Testament has now spread to all believers. As the passion of the fire forced Moses from his hiding place in the desert, the passion of the flames of fire carries the disciples out of the closed room into the streets. As Moses preached to the Israelites and to Pharaoh, so the disciples of Pentecost preach to people of every tongue.

In this brief survey of biblical passages we see God's passion manifest as fire. In the Old Testament, God—visible as fire—argues, leads, fights, and consumes offerings as well as enemies. Fire is a towering, raging, protective, and comforting presence. The New Testament passages about fire begin with similar force. The image of John the Baptist, raging with fire's passion and threatening unquenchable punishment on the hypocritical priests, holds more of the judgment of the irascible Hebrew prophets than the compassion of Jesus. The passionate force of the Old Testament fire takes on the risk of incarnation, not only into the Word and Son, but astonishingly into his disciples as well. In Jesus and through his ministry shining passion no longer belongs exclusively to YHWH Elohim arguing from the burning bush with Moses, but also to the Spirit descending as tongues of fire, speaking through the disciples. In the first stories God was fire. In the latter stories fire is dispersed, as all Christ's followers are challenged to burn with the passion of God.

FIRE IN THE BAPTISMAL TRADITION

Passionate, radiant God,
  Make us vibrant with your gift of fire in baptism.
Fire of God,
  Consume our offerings,
  Purify our love,
  Illumine the world.

Patristic Understanding of Fire In Baptism

This section of the sacramental story of fire explores patristic insights into fire—both flame and light—that led to the lighted candle of baptism.

As in the two previous chapters, we begin with Kilian McDonnell's investigation into the patristic teachings of fire in the baptism of Jesus. We then turn to the ritual history of fire by exploring the significance of the paschal candle and the blessings of fire at the Easter Vigil.

Significance of Fire in Jesus' Baptism

In his work, *The Baptism of Jesus in the Jordan*, Kilian McDonnell addresses fire in the baptism of Jesus as both flame and light.[26] As flame, fire is both judgment and sanctification. As light, fire is the glory of God that brings illumination to the baptized. Writing about fire as flame, Justin Martyr says in his *Dialogue with Trypho*, "As Jesus went down into the water, the Jordan was set ablaze." McDonnell suggests that Justin may have developed this extratextual idea from early sources such as *The Preaching of Paul*, which says, "When [Jesus] was baptized, fire appeared upon the water."[27] Another source of Justin's image may have been the words of John the Baptist, who warns that Jesus will baptize with the Holy Spirit and fire. In this context fire carries the threat of judgment.

Developing the idea of fire sanctifying the waters, Jacob of Serugh uses the image of the purifying coal of Isaiah (6:6). In his telling, the burning coal that once purified the unclean lips of the prophet is now personified by Christ entering the Jordan. He tells us that Christ went into the Jordan as a coal whose fire ignited flames of sanctifying power over the water. Once purified and ablaze, the Jordan became the refining furnace in which the baptized are restored to purity.

Shifting focus from flame to fire's glow, McDonnell turns to Ephrem the Syrian (ca. 306–373) and Gregory of Nazianzus (ca. 329–390). Ephrem teaches that Mary shares the same splendorous light as the Jordan because they both held the Savior in their wombs. Christ himself is the radiance that imparts divine light. For Ephrem there are only two light-bearers, Mary and the Jordan. They alone hold the fullness of divine light; however, the light also dwells externally on Moses and other luminaries of the scriptural narrative. Gregory of Nazianzus extends this possession of light to all the baptized. In the *Oration on the Holy Lights*, a sermon given on the feast of the Epiphany and followed by baptism, he says, "Christ is illumined: let us burn bright." He likens John the Baptist to a

---

26. Kilian McDonnell, *The Baptism of Jesus in the Jordan: The Trinitarian and Cosmic Order of Salvation* (Collegeville, MN: Liturgical Press, 1996), 106–10.

27. Ibid., 106.

lamp and Jesus to the Sun. The brilliance of this Sun is assisted by the "perfect light" of the baptized, who are "as stars in the world."[28]

Instructions and Blessings of Fire

The practice of giving a lighted candle to the newly baptized draws on an understanding of Christ as the light and the baptized as participants in that same Christ-light. The tradition of relating baptism to light, even calling it illumination, dates to the first generations of Christians. In the letter to the Hebrews the author exhorts the community to persevere in spite of trials. They are told: "Remember the great challenge of the sufferings that you had to meet after you received the light [at baptism]" (Heb 10:32). John Chrysostom (ca. 347–407) refers to the letter to the Ephesians in a homily addressed to the recently baptized, saying: "Awake, you who are asleep, wash yourself among the dead and Christ will be your illumination [Eph 5:14]." The *Didascalia of the Twelve Apostles* (ca. 250) teaches: "as soon as you have believed and have been baptized, a great light has shone upon you." In his *Oration on Holy Baptism*, Gregory of Nazianzus writes that the first light given to the people was the Law. The lamp of the Law guided the people throughout history until the true light was made manifest in Bethlehem. Moreover, he teaches, "baptismal illumination is more properly still a light. It expels the devil who is darkness and a counterfeit of the light." Gregory continues by saying that Christ is the fire who purifies, who brings "light and with it joy, light's companion."[29]

Although there is a reference to receiving a lighted candle at baptism in Ambrose's *On the Fall of Consecrated Virgins* (ca. 390), we have no record of early liturgies containing this practice.[30] One reason for this might be that the Easter Vigil, when baptisms were traditionally celebrated, began after dark. In the early church, centuries before the advent of gas or electric lights, everyone would have carried candles to help illumine the church. Receiving a candle lit from the Easter fire may have had practical as well as symbolic origins.

28. Ibid., 109.

29. Philip Schaff and Henry Wace, eds., *Nicene and Post-Nicene Fathers*, 2d ed. (New York: Hendrickson, 1999), 7:360–78.

30. Herbert Thurston, "Paschal Candle," *The Catholic Encyclopedia*, ed. Charles Herbermann, Conde Pallen, Thomas Shahan, and John Wynne, 515–16 (New York: Appleton, 1911).

Prior to consistent evidence for the baptismal candle, the paschal candle was clearly in use. The earliest reference to the paschal candle occurs in a letter Jerome wrote in 384 in response to a request to write a *carmen cerei* or song for the candle. Although Jerome refused, the request verifies the existence of the paschal candle by at least the latter half of the fourth century. The next piece of evidence for the candle comes from Augustine, who mentions that he wrote a *carmen*. The role of lighting the candle belonged to a deacon, so it is likely that he wrote his *carmen* before 391, the year he was ordained a bishop. A *carmen cerei* is also found in the writings of Magnus Felix Ennodius (ca. 474–521).

Ennodius's song added new layers of significance to the paschal candle. Already in the prayers the paschal candle, a tall column of wax, was likened to the pillar of fire that led the Israelites from slavery to the Promised Land. Similarly, during the Easter Vigil this paschal fire symbolically recapitulates that journey as it leads the people from the darkness of Friday to the glory of Sunday. The candle also signified a burnt offering, not only the offering of the people at this liturgy but also the offering of Jesus himself on Calvary. The candle was often inscribed with a cross and an image of Jesus' wounds symbolically marked with incense. To this symbolism Ennodius added the three elements of the candle itself: the wax, the wick, and the light. The wax—believed to be produced by virgin bees—symbolized the purity of Jesus' body, born of a virgin. The papyrus wick, which grew in water along riverbeds, recalled the water hallowed by Jesus' baptism. Finally, the flame represented the burning bush. For Ennodius the paschal candle represents "the God-hallowed material world, and by extension the whole of creation, which as a result of the Incarnation and the advent of the end-time following the Resurrection, has now become potentially redeemable. Therefore, the offering of the Candle, this microcosm of the world, would symbolize and once more re-enact the union of heaven and Earth in anticipation of the final redemption of all creation at the close of the Age."[31] The candles currently received by the newly baptized are in the lineage of this cosmic and biblical fullness of the paschal candle.

From instructions and insights into fire in the baptismal tradition, we turn now to blessings used in ancient liturgies. Relying once again on Paul Palmer's work in *Sacraments and Worship*, we find that the Gelasian

---

31. A. J. MacGregor, *Fire and Light in the Western Triduum: Their Use at Tenebrae and at the Paschal Vigil* (Collegeville, MN: Liturgical Press, 1992), 303.

Sacramentary does not have a blessing of the new fire.[32] Instead, the Easter Vigil began with a litany to the saints followed by the "Lamb of God." When this prayer is concluded, "an arch-deacon comes in front of the altar, receives a light from fire that was hid away on Friday, makes the sign of the cross on the candle, and lighting it, brings the ceremony to a close by personally blessing it."[33]

Later in the Vigil the presider sang the *Deus mundi Conditor* (God, Maker of the World), an Easter hymn of praise. This hymn ended with a formal blessing of the candle:

> Almighty God, pour out your abundant blessing upon this lighted candle. O invisible renewer of life, look with favor upon this lamp of night so that the sacrifice offered this eve may marvelously reflect your own light, and let the power of your majesty drive out the deceits of Satan and remain wherever this blessed holy fire may be taken. Through Christ our Lord. Amen.[34]

The Gelasian liturgy continued with the blessing of the font for baptism. In this blessing the lighted paschal candle is dipped in the water three times while the priest says: "May the power of the Holy Ghost descend into this brimming font. And may it make the whole substance of this water fruitful in regenerative power."[35] With the water blessed, the liturgy continues with the baptismal ceremony, but that ceremony does not include the reception of a lighted candle.

The oldest known blessing of fire dates approximately to 1000. Found in the Easter liturgy of Benevento, a city in southern Italy, this most ancient blessing is the source of the one used today. In Benevento the Easter Vigil started with the lighting of the fire and the prayer: "O God, through your Son, the cornerstone, you bestowed the light of your glory upon the faithful. Sanctify † this new fire which was struck from flint and

32. Paul F. Palmer, ed., *Sacraments and Worship: Liturgy and Doctrinal Development of Baptism, Confirmation, and the Eucharist*, Sources of Christian Theology 1 (Westminster, MD: Newman Press, 1955), 31.

33. Ibid., 31.

34. H. A. Wilson, ed., *The Gelasian Sacramentary: Liber Sacramentorum Romanae Ecclesiae* (Oxford: Clarendon Press, 1894), 81. Translated in *The English-Latin Sacramentary for the United States of America; the Prayers of the Celebrant of Mass Together with the Ordinary of the Mass* (New York: Catholic Book Publishing. Co., 1966), 104.

35. Palmer, ed., *Sacraments and Worship*, 37.

is destined for our use. Grant that we may be so inflamed with heavenly desires through this paschal feast that we may come to the feast of eternal light with pure minds. Through Christ our Lord. Amen."[36]

Other early blessings are similar in form to this prayer, but vary in response to regional customs. In some locations, as in the Gelasian community, a new fire was not lighted, but was reserved from Friday. In other places the Vigil started early in the day and the fire was lit with a magnifying lens. However and whenever it was kindled, the fire atop the paschal candle was the most prominent symbol of the Easter Vigil.

The ancient texts reviewed in this brief summary of the patristic understandings of fire in baptism are the source of the contemporary blessings of fire and candles of the Easter Vigil. There is scant mention of giving the newly baptized a ritually lighted candle in these texts, perhaps because of reliance on candlelight to illumine the evening Vigil; all members of the congregation, including the baptismal candidates, would have held candles throughout the celebration. Unlike the blessings of water and oil, which come to the current Sacramentary directly from the Gelasian Sacramentary, we have seen that the blessing of fire and the use of a lighted candle in baptism have a less direct route. Although there was local variation in the use of fire in the Vigil, the blessing of fire currently in use is the Beneventian prayer and the blessing of the paschal candle is the remnant of a Gelasian Easter hymn. Adherence to the ancient blessings reveals the lack of influence that scientific insights into fire, especially fire as light, exercised on the theological appreciation of fire as a sacramental.[37] For that reason we continue the sacramental story of fire with the current blessings of the new fire and the paschal candle at the Easter Vigil, the presentation of a lighted candle to the newly baptized, and the instructions concerning fire in the *Catechism*.

Contemporary Understanding of Fire in Baptism

The contemporary Easter Vigil begins with fire. After dark, at the doors of the church, a fire is kindled, the paschal candle is lighted, and

---

36. MacGregor, *Fire and Light in the Western Triduum: Their Use at Tenebrae and at the Paschal Vigil*, 158, 457, translated in *The English-Latin Sacramentary*, 102.

37. For a history of the development of knowledge about light see Arthur Zajonc, *Catching the Light: The Entwined History of Light and Mind* (Oxford: Oxford University Press, 1993).

from it participants in the celebration light tapers and thus fill the entire church with light. Eventually electric lights are turned on and the tapers are extinguished. Later in the service, candles are lighted from the paschal candle and presented to each of the newly baptized. Continuous with ancient tradition, fire signifies God's presence and the light of Christ, which all members of the church share. As noted above, the prayer used to bless the new fire derives from a blessing written before the year 1000. Not surprisingly, there is no longer mention of flint. The priest begins:

> Father,
> we share in the light of your glory
> through your Son, the light of the world.
> Make this new fire † holy, and inflame us with new hope.
> Purify our minds by this Easter celebration
> and bring us one day to the feast of eternal light. (9)[38]

After the fire is lighted and blessed, the priest etches a cross in the wax with a stylus. He then inscribes the candle with an alpha, an omega, and the numerals of the year, and inserts five grains of incense. Once the candle is prepared, he lights the candle from the new fire, saying:

> May the light of Christ, rising in glory,
> dispel the darkness of our hearts and minds. (11)

The deacon then lifts the candle and sings, "Christ is our light," to which the congregation responds, "Thanks be to God." Each member of the congregation then lights a taper from the paschal candle and moves into the darkened church. The paschal candle is solemnly carried into the church by the deacon, who stops twice to sing, "Christ is our light." Once the candle is placed in the sanctuary, the lights are turned on and the tapers held by the congregation are extinguished. The celebration continues with the Exultet, the Easter proclamation sung by the deacon. This proclamation exhorts the angels, the Earth, and the church to exult in glory because Jesus Christ, the King, is risen. The song then tells the story of salvation history and continues with praises of God's glory. The Easter Vigil then continues with the Liturgy of the Word, which is a

---

38. *The Rites of the Catholic Church*, vol. 1 (Collegeville, MN: Liturgical Press, 1990).

series of readings, psalms, and canticles from both the Old and the New Testaments that tell the biblical story of salvation.

After the Liturgy of the Word, the celebration continues with the blessing of the font for baptism. In this blessing the lighted paschal candle is dipped in the water three times while, with words based on the Gelasian Sacramentary, the priest says:

> We ask you, Father, with your Son
> to send the Holy Spirit upon the waters of this font.
> May all who are buried with Christ in the death of baptism
> rise also with him to newness of life. (311)

Once all those presented for baptism have been washed in water, anointed with oil, and dressed in a white garment, the presider invites their godparents to light a candle from the paschal candle and present it to the newly baptized. The presider then says:

> You have been enlightened by Christ.
> Walk always as children of the light
> and keep the flame of faith alive in your hearts.
> When the Lord comes, may you go out to meet him
> with all the saints in the heavenly kingdom. Amen. (361)

The celebration continues with confirmation, after which the new members of the church blow out their candles and return to their seats.

By now it can be no surprise that the current ritual use of fire derives from the ancient rubrics. The blessings of fire, despite the use of matches in place of flint, repeat the same themes, and the deacon remains the minister of the candle, which is still inscribed with a cross. In current practice the Gelasian blessing of the paschal candle is omitted and replaced with the preparation of the candle, the roots of which are equally old. The presentation of the lighted candle to the newly baptized—an uncertainly attested practice in the ancient ritual—is codified here. The advent of electric lights may have instigated the standardization of the ancient insight linking baptism as illumination to candlelight.

From the blessing and prayers of the current Sacramentary, we turn now to the *Catechism of the Catholic Church* for instructions about fire, light, and candles. Without reference to modern discoveries about light, these teachings remain unchanged since the early days of the church. In its section on "The Names, Titles, and Symbols of the Holy Spirit,"[39] the *Catechism* instructs that

> fire symbolizes the transforming energy of the Holy Spirit's actions. The prayer of the prophet Elijah, who "arose like fire" and whose "word burned like a torch," brought down fire from heaven on the sacrifice on Mount Carmel [*Sir* 48:1; cf. *1 Kings* 18:38-39]. This event was a "figure" of the fire of the Holy Spirit, who transforms what he touches. John the Baptist, who goes "before [the Lord] in the spirit and power of Elijah," proclaims Christ as the one who "will baptize you with the Holy Spirit and with fire" [*Lk* 1:17; 3:16]. . . . In the form of tongues "as of fire," the Holy Spirit rests on the disciples on the morning of Pentecost and fills them with himself [*Acts* 2:3-4]. The spiritual tradition has retained this symbolism of fire as one of the most expressive images of the Holy Spirit's actions. (696)

Following this passage on fire, the *Catechism* continues with light as a symbol of the Spirit. Combining cloud and light, it teaches:

> These two images occur together in the manifestations of the Holy Spirit. In theophanies of the Old Testament, the cloud, now obscure, now luminous, reveals the living and saving God, while veiling the transcendence of his glory—with Moses on Mount Sinai [cf. *Ex* 24:15-18], at the tent of meeting [cf. *Ex* 33:9-10], and during the wandering in the desert [cf. *Ex* 40:36-38; *1 Cor* 10:1-2], and with Solomon at the dedication of the Temple [cf. *1 Kings* 8:10-12]. In the Holy Spirit, Christ fulfills these figures. . . . On the mountain of Transfiguration, the Spirit in the "cloud came and overshadowed" Jesus, Moses and Elijah, Peter, James and John, and "a voice came out of the cloud, saying, 'This is my Son, my Chosen; listen to him!'" [*Lk* 9:34-35]. (697)

The *Catechism* also quotes Justin Martyr, teaching that baptism is called enlightenment "because those who receive this [catechetical] instruction are enlightened in their understanding." Having received baptism, they become children of light, and indeed "light" themselves (1216). Finally, referring to the presentation of the lighted candle, the *Catechism* says: "The candle, lit from the Easter candle, signifies that Christ has enlightened the neophyte [or newly baptized]. In him the baptized are 'the light of the world'" [*Mt* 5:14; cf. *Phil* 2:15] (1243).

39. CCC, Part One, Section 2, Chapter 3, Article 8.

The instructions concerning fire in the *Catechism* mention its transformative and luminous qualities. Drawing from Scripture and tradition, they offer insight into the power and dynamism of fire. The less obvious qualities of fire that derive from its natural history, including its origin, electromagnetic resonance with the Sun and stars as well as all matter, and its similarity to respiration are not included. Even without this modern knowledge, the church reveals an intuitive sense of the pervasiveness of fire by using a lighted candle to symbolize a heart aflame with faith and by insisting that all believers are light for the world.

We have now completed the sacramental story of fire in the Roman Catholic tradition. We have followed this story through Scriptures, blessings, and instructions to baptismal candidates. We saw Old Testament images of fire that caused Moses to cover his face in fear and then sent him as a prophet to Pharaoh. We then saw God as a fire that destroyed enemies and consumed offerings. Then came the glory of God as the unbearable light that filled the temple and drove the priests out. The New Testament starts with an image of the messiah as one who will judge with fire. Stories of Jesus, however, seem to temper the ferocity of fire. When Jesus is transfigured on the mountaintop with the glory of the light that filled the temple the disciples fall to the ground in fear, but instead of driving them away Jesus reassures them and tells them not to be afraid. Jesus reveals himself as the light and insists that his followers are also lights he encourages to shine brightly. As if to complete a circle, the Holy Spirit falls upon the disciples at Pentecost in tongues of flame. Once again God is speaking through fire, this time not in a bush that does not burn, but through disciples who burn with passion.

Fire also manifests God as an approachable light in the liturgy, where we encountered flame and light as both purifying and illuminating. In the Easter Vigil the majesty of God fills the church, no longer to drive priests out but as candlelight carried by the people. At the end of this progression toward gentleness, the light given to the newly baptized is candle flame symbolizing the light they are called to tend within themselves. Interestingly, the final rubric of the current baptismal ritual instructs the baptized to blow out their candles. This seems to be in contradiction to the admonition they have just heard to "keep the flame of faith alive in [their] hearts." Unfortunately, there is nothing yet in the current rite to reveal the connection of the extinguishable candle flame to the unquenchable fire that constantly burns in their hearts. However, because of the vivacious nature of fire, the brevity of its blessings, and its significance in the Easter Vigil, the power of fire as a sacramental for baptism has not diminished. Somehow, the ease of turning an electric switch has not evacuated light or fire of its majesty or mystery. Unlike its modern substitutes, however, fire is unpredictable. The domestic nature of a candle flame is not to be taken for granted. A single spark still ignites a wildfire. Because fire transforms all it touches, a tended heart flame has the potential to transform a life.

COSMOCENTRIC SACRAMENTALITY AND FIRE

Once again we have traveled 13.7 billion years through the story of a sacramental. We began the story of fire on Earth as the conditions for fire emerged. We saw that both the oxygen and the fuel required for fire were provided by photosynthetic beings that split water molecules and released oxygen into the atmosphere. Millions of years later they were joined by land plants that provided fuel as well as oxygen. Through the resonance with the Sun developed by photosynthetic creatures, fire ignited and Earth created light. After the emergence of fire we followed the story of the domestication of fire from wildfires to candlelight. We then paused to notice how fire appears in our own bodies and learned that our respiration, indeed the respiration of all animals, involves the same process as the flame of a candle. We also learned that we radiate light like a candle and are held in an electromagnetic embrace.[40] Although the cosmic story of fire begins on Earth, it reaches back in time to the Beginning through the origins of creatures on Earth, the formation of the Sun and Solar System, and through fire's electromagnetic lineage.

In the sacramental story we saw fire manifest God. As both flame and light, God consumed, guided, judged, overwhelmed, and remained present. In the course of the story we saw fire shift from the fearsome sight of God's presence, to Jesus and his followers as the light of the world, to the candles of the Easter Vigil and baptism. Both the natural

40. For an insightful study on the spiritual significance of electromagnetism see Lawrence W. Fagg, *Electromagnetism and the Sacred: At the Frontier of Spirit and Matter* (New York: Continuum, 1999).

history and the sacramental stories suggest an increasing gentleness of fire, although the danger of wildfire and the awesome power of God still cloak themselves in the coy glow of a candle. Reflection on the stories of fire can reawaken a baptismal candidate to the glory of God that permeates creation. Moreover, integrating the natural history and sacramental stories of fire forms part of the foundation of a cosmocentric sacramentality.

The concept of thresholds developed by Pierre Teilhard de Chardin is useful for the integration of the natural history and sacramental stories of fire. As we have seen, Teilhard divided Earth's history into four phases—pre-life, life, thought, and superlife. The pre-life phase of fire begins with the birth of the Universe and the electromagnetic force. It shines through the radiance of stars. Fire crosses the threshold into the life phase when living beings first respond to the enriched atmosphere by breathing oxygen. Without a flame, combustion begins with respiration in living beings.

Some three billion years later, after wildfires repeatedly charred continents, fire jumped the threshold into the phase of thought when humans began to wonder about fire. Paleolithic people used fire for domestic purposes such as illumination and cooking. Their ability to carry fire enabled them to migrate into colder climates. Many thousands of years later, Neolithic people with fire-making technologies extended the use of fire to such purposes as agriculture and metallurgy. Many thousands of years later, inventors learned to harness fire's power in internal combustion engines and triggered the Industrial Revolution. The machines of the modern era required massive amounts of fuel. The generosity of the plants, which supply the oxygen and the fuel for fire, is becoming exhausted as forests are cut, coal mined, and oil drilled. Only recently, as we recognize that we are choking on the exhaust of our factories, power plants, and cars, have we begun to realize that our use of fire has become abusive not only to ourselves, but to the entire Earth community.

The threshold into the superlife phase of fire is crossed not when we begin to address the damage humans have caused by fire, but when we begin to realize that we are fire. Our consciousness is fueled by fire. Teilhard de Chardin tells us: "Some say, after we have mastered the wind, the waves, the tides, and gravity, we shall harness for God the energies of love. Then for the second time in the history of the world, [humans] will have discovered fire."[41] Our love, our passion is fueled by fire. Moreover, in

41. Pierre Teilhard de Chardin, *Toward the Future* (New York: Harcourt Brace Jovanovich, 1975), 87.

the superlife phase of fire we come to know that the fire burning within us, physically and spiritually, burns in all living things. Everything is fire. Fire—flame and light—resonant with Sun and stars, provides the energy that courses through all that breathes and holds the entire world together at the most intimate level. We are fire in its superlife phase as we learn to recognize the common flame within each being and as we strive to become increasingly receptive to the light each one continually radiates. In its superlife phase fire has the transformative power to draw our attention, argue us past our fear, impassion us, and guide us to fullness of life for ourselves and love and passion for the entire Earth community. The flame is there. We have only to tend it.

In summary, we may say that through these developmental stages the emphasis in the story of fire shifts from the inorganic, to the living, to human thought, and finally to the conscious knowledge that the entire cosmos is alight with dancing flames. In this final stage we experience ourselves not only in our particular human line of descent but also in a radiant lineage that illumines the cosmos and binds it together. Teilhard's concept of thresholds in Earth's development places the aware person within the radiant glow of the natural history and sacramental story of fire.

What might this awareness of oneself as glowing with fire's story mean to a person as she is presented with a lighted candle at baptism? In her cosmocentric perspective at least three insights might occur. The first thing she is likely to notice is the appropriateness of blowing out the candle flame so soon after she receives it. This apparent irony of extinguishing the fire while keeping it burning in her heart makes better sense when seen in a cosmocentric light. She has learned through the natural history of fire that the flame in her heart cannot go out until her death and even then, after the fire of respiration ceases, electromagnetic light will perpetually radiate from the matter that formed her body. She has also learned that through baptism she has been enlightened by Christ. She is a light that cannot be extinguished. The candle she is given, a small version of the paschal candle, represents the divine and human natures of Jesus the Christ lived as an offering to God. She recalls that Ennodius took this image further and taught that the candle also represents the union of the divine with creation. The reception of her candle represents her personal participation in the mystery of the incarnation and self-offering. Light and joy mingle and she knows she is as radiant as the candle.

As she realizes herself as unquenchable flame she might take comfort in knowing that she is not alone. She may feel a little giddy as she looks around her in the church and is dazzled by the light shining from so many sources. She might drop her eyes in an attempt to veil herself from the press of light she feels all around her and welling up within her. Keeping the flame alive in her heart, she begins to understand, is about tending this flame that cannot go out, as well as learning to notice the same flame in all members of the Earth community. She might recall Pierre Teilhard de Chardin's "Mass on the World" and bring to mind his image of the radiance of the Host spreading out across all of creation.[42] She knows that Earth does not need to be offered to God again and again because the truth of Teilhard's vision is already embedded in every cell and every atom. God glows within creation. The consecration is complete. At her baptism she receives a diminutive candle flame, but as she looks up with joy she sees the bonfire, the wildfire of which she is a part.

Another insight that might occur to her is the lesson fire teaches about intimacy. The scientific story of fire moves from raging forest fires and a Sun that cannot be looked at directly to domestic fire and candle flames that draw her gaze, and even to all the Earth quietly ablaze. The sacred story is similar. It moves from fearsome theophanies to Jesus transfigured, saying "fear not," to candles as signs of God's presence, and even to herself as light. Meditating on all this as God revealed in fire, she might consider a pattern of experiences common to deepening intimacy with God. As intimacy grows, a child's fear of God as a stern parent often turns to the comfort of Jesus as a friend. This closeness may yield to the joy of God as lover and then, with further spiritual maturity, melt into the oneness of mystical intimacy. In each of these stories—the cosmic, the sacramental, and the personal—the unapproachable becomes inseparable from herself. Presented her candle at baptism, she might pause as she recalls that Moses' story began with his attraction to a fire. She may well hesitate as she wonders where this small flame, taken into her heart, will lead her. As she teeters between attraction and fear, she may wonder if this fire she holds is the source that draws the entire Universe forward and all she need do to be part of that majestic sweep is follow the unquenchable fire in her heart.

A Hymn to Fire

> *Passionate, radiant God,*
> *Make us vibrant with your gift of fire in baptism.*

---

42. Pierre Teilhard de Chardin, "Mass on the World," in idem, *The Heart of Matter* (New York: Harcourt Brace Jovanovich, 1978), 119–34.

Fire born of stars and Earth,
Life-air dance that stabilized the atmosphere,
Burning within and not consuming,
Illuminating, embracing energy, universal bond

Flame and light
Warmth and caves
Fire of torches, and candles, and lamps
Lighting, heating, fighting, comforting

Passion of God and Moses
Burning bush and blazing pillar
Sending, guiding
Destroying enemies, accepting offerings, and ourselves

Light of the world
Stars, and Son, and us,
Light in darkness and in day,
Candles called to set the world ablaze.

Fire of God,
Consume our offerings,
Purify our love,
Illumine the world.

Passionate and radiant God,
Make us vibrant with your gift of fire in baptism.

Chapter Four

COSMOCENTRIC SACRAMENTALITY

The integration of the scientific and sacred stories of the sacramentals leads to a cosmocentric understanding of sacramentality. In this chapter we explore the significance of the stories of water, oil, and fire for baptism and then extend these insights to the seven ritual sacraments and to sacramentality in general. This chapter is presented in two sections. The first, "Baptism," gathers the themes and insights suggested by the integration of the cosmic and sacramental stories of water, oil, and fire. It continues with a reflection on Trinity suggested by the sacramentals and concludes with a cosmocentric consideration of baptism. The second section, "Sacramentality," begins with a consideration of sacramentals in rituals and leads to the unique role of the human in a God-drenched Universe.

BAPTISM

Each of the previous three chapters concludes with a reflection on the integration of the scientific and sacred stories of a sacramental. We now turn to a consideration of what these reflections reveal about the cosmocentric celebration of baptism. To address this question we first gather the key points from the previous chapters. We then consider what water, oil, and fire reveal about God. Next, we follow baptism through the four Teilhardian developmental thresholds from a pre-life through a cosmocentric perspective. Finally, we conclude this section with a reflection on the cosmocentric celebration of baptism itself.

Reflections from Water, Oil, and Fire

The previous three chapters traced the stories of water, oil, and fire from their cosmic origins to their presence in the body of the person celebrating baptism. In each chapter the story of one sacramental was told, beginning with biblical accounts and concluding with current teachings. Each set of stories was integrated in light of Teilhard de Chardin's thresholds in Earth's development. Finally, the significance of the integration of the stories was considered from the perspective of a person about to be baptized. As we look back on those reflections, four key points emerge. First, the scientific and sacred stories of each sacramental are complementary; in each case the two stories deepen and support each other. Second, the stories all point to the essential sacredness of the world. Third, there is continuity: the stories of each sacramental are continuous with the story of the person preparing for baptism. Fourth, compassion: the person being baptized realizes that she is invited to feel deeply the joys and sorrows of the Earth community.

Complementarity

The scientific stories of water, oil, and fire complement their sacred stories. Any concern that the science might contradict the sacred tradition is unfounded. Rather than raising doubts about the use of a sacramental, in each case the scientific exploration lends support to ancient wisdom. Neither does a scientific appreciation of a sacramental diminish its mystery. Instead, by integrating the two stories of each baptismal sacramental we reclaim lost bits of knowledge, add new information that has never been available to sacramental reflection, and trace the mysterious gifts of each sacramental back to the beginning of time. Noticing that the cosmic and sacred stories of sacramentals complement each other is an initial step toward a cosmocentric celebration of baptism.

The scientific and sacramental stories of water show complementarity. In both stories water is essential in creating and sustaining life. The scientific story tells us that water is involved in every form of birth. From the stars to the Earth, to the first life on Earth, and to each life thereafter, water is part of birth. All living beings are born in water and sustained by water. Additionally, water nurtures life by carrying nutrients to cells and washing away their waste. Water is the matrix of all cellular activity. Each living being and the planet as a whole is constantly bathed and renewed by water. The scientific story of water as the agent of birth and cleansing resonates with ancient sacramental wisdom.

There is also a resonance between the scientific and sacred stories of oil. From the sacred story we know that oil in baptism makes the presence of God visible and expresses divine favor. From the cosmic story we recall that the presence of oil in membranes was essential for life to begin on Earth. An oily membrane surrounds each cell, protecting it while keeping it in constant communication with its environment. The membrane that surrounds our bodies is our skin. The oil in skin protects it and makes it shine just as oil used to dedicate sacred vessels prevents tarnishing and makes them shine. In addition to membranes, oil in plants feeds and sustains animal life. Fruit-bearing plants, with olive trees as an exemplar, generously give their rich fruit to nourish the beasts and birds with whom they have coevolved intricate relationships. The omnipresence of oil, its generosity, protection, and relationality, occurs in both the cosmic and sacred stories.

The scientific and sacramental stories of fire are also complementary. Fire in baptism symbolizes the light of Christ and the flame of the Spirit that is to be kept burning within the heart of each baptized person. From the scientific story we learn that each cell burns with the same process as the lighted candle presented at baptism. Moreover, every bit of matter constantly radiates light. That constant presence of light is the living flame of the Spirit received at baptism, which can never be extinguished. Although there are others, these examples alone are enough to put to rest any fear that the scientific and sacred stories of sacraments contradict each other.

Blessing

The second key point that emerges in these scientific and sacred stories is the blessed nature of the world. From the scientific stories we see the marvels of water, oil, and fire and how they make life possible. From the sacred stories we learn that the world is twice blessed and that the presence of God resides in each member of the Body of Christ. Recognizing the sacredness of every aspect of the cosmos is another step toward a cosmocentric approach to baptism.

The scientific story of water leaves no doubt in the faith-filled person that God's blessing is present in water. This blessing was present in the watery darkness that birthed our Sun and in the ocean womb that nurtured the first life. Since the oceans formed, God's blessing has fallen with the rain that soaks dry roots and allows fruit and those who feast on it to thrive. Divine blessing is present in the water that slakes thirst and rushes to every cell in a body with the nutrients it needs. God's blessing, which creates and sustains life, is carried and manifested by water.

In the sacramental story of water a strong biblical and patristic tradition holds that everything created enjoys God's blessing. At the end of each day of creation God proclaimed everything made that day good. God delights in creation. That initial blessing was lost, according to patristic teachings, when Adam and Eve sinned and were expelled from the Garden. This fate suffered by Adam and Eve was shared by all creation. After many generations God's blessing was restored to both humanity and creation at Jesus' baptism. *The Teaching of St. Gregory* (ca. 490) declares that water everywhere rippled in response to the divine touch of Jesus' feet as he entered the water of the Jordan. Through the water of Jesus' baptism God's blessing once again flowed into creation.

The stories of oil also show the sacredness of creation. From the scientific story we recall that oil provided the cradle in which the first life on Earth formed. Without the blessing of an oily membrane to protect it, nascent life would not have survived Earth's turbulent oceans. The membranes that separate cells and beings from one another also carry God's blessing of sensitivity. The gift of receptivity and response is given to living beings through oily membranes. God's blessing is also manifest in the sacrifice of plants that give themselves to the animal community as food. God's blessing is particularly manifest in the generosity of olive trees.

In the sacramental story of oil we learned of Irenaeus's concept of the two anointings. Both of these anointings are blessings that convey God's presence and favor. Irenaeus teaches that the first anointing occurred as God anointed the world with the Word as the world was created. Each being received the christic presence and was called good. The second anointing was the descent of the Spirit upon Jesus at his baptism. This anointing was accompanied by the proclamation of Jesus as the Beloved. Irenaeus tells us that although the Spirit was already present to Jesus, he received this anointing in order to communicate the Spirit to others, and that all humanity and all creation shared in this anointing of Jesus' human nature. Through these two anointings the world is twice blessed.

The scientific and sacred stories of fire also tell us about God's blessing manifest in the world. In the previous chapter the scientific story explored fire in terms of flame and light and related these to respiration and electromagnetism, respectively. Recall that as a candle burns it oxidizes the hydrocarbons in the wax vapor. A process similar to that occurring visibly in a flame also occurs in the respiration of cells. God's blessing of breath is sustained by this fiery metabolism. Electromagnetism is the interaction that holds everything together at the atomic and molecular level. If this interaction relaxed for just a second the entire Universe would dissipate into particles smaller than dust. As this bond holds particles together it interacts with photons of light in such a way that everything is constantly absorbing and radiating light. Electromagnetism is one of the glues through which God holds the world together. It carries God's blessing of creation as well as the blessing of light.

In the sacred story of fire we notice the decentralization of fire as an image of the presence of God. In the Old Testament fire as both flame and light convey God's presence. God calls to Moses from the burning bush, leads the chosen people with a pillar of fire, devours the sacrifice of a faithful prophet, and floods the temple with the light of divine glory. In the New Testament and early Christian tradition fire as light became a symbol of Christ, and fire as flame became a symbol of the presence of the Spirit. Jesus was transfigured before his disciples. Starlight guided people to him at his birth and sunlight faltered at his death. Candlelight represents the light of Christ at the Easter Vigil. Simultaneously, fire as flame manifests the Spirit that descends upon the disciples at Pentecost and is the symbol of the presence of the Spirit the baptized are called to tend in their hearts. Initially, the symbol of fire was used to represent the awesome nature of God that is distinct from creation. Eventually fire came to represent the incarnate blessing of God and even the presence of God within the faithful. To continue this extension into a cosmocentric perspective, fire as flame and light represents, as do water and oil, the blessing of God present throughout the entire cosmos.

Continuity

The third point that emerges from the integration of the scientific and sacred stories of water, oil, and fire is the underlying unity of the person being baptized with the entire Earth community. Each of the sacramentals has a story that reaches back to the Beginning, extends to all living things, and also embraces the baptismal candidate.

The cosmic story of water indicates that every living being is connected by water. Each being participates in the hydrological cycle that circulates water around the planet. The birth and life of each being relies on water, as do the metabolic processes of each living cell. The water on Earth sustains and is shared by all life on the planet. The sacramental story of water declares that all water, including the water that comprises

70 percent of a person's body, was blessed by God during the first days of creation and that the blessing recurred when Jesus stepped into the waters of the Jordan. Because she is made of water more than anything else, and because she relies on water for everything she does, the person being baptized can recognize the continuity between herself and both the cosmic and sacred stories of water.

Drawing once again on Irenaeus, we learn that the entire world was anointed when it was created and again when the Spirit descended on Jesus at his baptism. Through patristic teaching we learn that all creation is twice blessed. Additionally, we learn from the cosmic story that all beings have oily membranes and that all animals have oils in their skin. The presence of oil enables the sensitivity and receptivity that flows through the Earth community. Aware of the stories of oil, the person being baptized knows that the glow of her skin and her ability to respond to sensation are part of the unfolding story of the Universe becoming increasingly aware of itself.

From the cosmic story of fire we learned that flame glows within each living being and all matter radiates light. Furthermore, the plasma in flame is the only naturally occurring condition on Earth that approximates that of stellar cores and the early period of the Universe's existence. In each of these places subatomic particles of matter reside at the threshold of radiant transformation. From the sacramental story of fire we learned that through baptism a person is illuminated. The lighted candle received by each person invites her to attend perpetually to the transformative presence of the Spirit. These stories of fire invite her to notice the light that swirls constantly around her and to dance with the Spirit that transforms the Universe.

Compassion

The fourth key point is that the compassion a person feels is a gift from the Universe. On Earth the story of compassion begins in oil. The first living beings were enveloped by oily membranes that facilitate the flow of nutrients into the cell and the elimination of wastes. Cellular membranes enable the cell to discern what is harmful and to be avoided, and what is beneficial and to be pursued. Single-celled beings with no sight or smell are able to follow density gradients that lead them to higher concentrations of food. This sensitivity, developed by the most primitive life-forms, is the origin of sensitivity in plants and animals as well as the foundation of our compassion. As we saw in the story of oil in our bodies, the cellular membranes, especially of our nervous systems, relay signals that allow us to interpret and respond to stimuli. The membranes of our eyes, nose, mouth, and ears all relay information for us to interpret. With this recognition of the significance of oil, the reception of oil at baptism takes on additional meaning for the newly baptized. Not only is it a sign of her anointing with the oil of gladness, it also signifies her deepening ability to share the joys of the entire community. Of course, sensitivity to joy is accompanied by an equal sensitivity to sorrow. Sensitivity, whether to joy, sorrow, or any of a host of possible feelings, elicits a response. By receiving oil at baptism a person is accepting the challenge to deepen in compassion and in the ability to respond to the Earth community.

As a baptismal candidate contemplates the sacramentals of baptism she notices that their scientific and sacred stories complement and support each other. She also realizes that she lives in a sacred, God-drenched Universe. More importantly, from a cosmocentric perspective, she comes to know the stories of the sacramentals as her own story. Through her baptism she is challenged to grow in compassion for the Earth community and invited into a deeper intimacy with the Universe and the God it reveals.

Reflections on Trinity

Water, oil, and fire lend themselves to a trinitarian reflection on God. Even though each divine person is distinct, it is in the nature of the Trinity to possess the fullness of each person of the Trinity within the other two persons. Any allegorical insights that could be correlated to one person could also be assigned to the other persons. In considering the stories of water, oil, and fire in baptism we could associate water with the Creator, oil with Christ, and fire with the Holy Spirit. The most apparent parallel is between Christ and oil. Although Jesus is anointed by the Spirit, "Christ" means the anointed, and through Christ the world is anointed. The Spirit, who is associated with each of these sacramentals, correlates most directly with fire. Although Jesus Christ is frequently referred to as the light of the world, light always signifies the presence of the Spirit. The fire of Pentecost, for example, represents the descent of the Spirit on the disciples. Finally, God the Creator aligns with water. Even though the Spirit is transformative in the waters of baptism, creation begins with water. Water is the matrix through which the Creator brings forth the world. Creator, Christ, and Spirit align with water, oil, and fire. With the dynamic nature of the Trinity in mind, we turn now to consider what the integration of the stories of the sacramentals reveals about the three persons of God.

The stories of water reflect God the Creator. As we saw, water is the source of all life. In the cosmic story, as soon as water emerges in the Universe it assists in birth and aids the ongoing creativity of the Universe. The creation of water is not told in the biblical story, but God's interaction with water initiates creation. The Spirit blows across the water and the Creator divides the waters in two. God chooses water as the matrix through which to create the Universe. Creation continues as water facilitates the Creator's blessing as every new life emerges. Water in its undifferentiated wholeness represents the Creator in the Trinity and carries the Creator's intention through biblical stories to the baptism of each person. Everything is born of water at the command of the first person of the Trinity, God, Creator, the source of all life and of all that is good.

Stories of oil suggest God the Son, the Christ who reveals the Father. As we saw in the cosmic stories, oil embraces every living cell. Irenaeus tells us that the world was anointed with the Word at its creation. It is through Christ the Anointed that all things come into being. The oil in each of our cells can be thought of as the presence of this primordial anointing. The story of the place of plants in the food chain and the generosity of flowering plants suggest a Christlike generosity. Jesus spoke of the grain of wheat that must fall to the ground and die in order to live. It is the lot of flowering plants such as wheat to be eaten or dispersed by animals so the plants can propagate. Olive seeds, in fact, require the softening provided by the digestion of animals in order to sprout. An olive that is not food for another simply dies. Remember that after Jesus offered his body and blood as bread and wine he endured the agony in Gethsemane, a name that actually means "olive press." Alongside images of sacrifice, oil reminds us of celebration. Ritual anointing with oil is a cause of joy and a sign of God's favor. When Jesus was anointed with the Spirit, a voice from heaven proclaimed him the beloved on whom God's favor rests. With Jesus the entire world is anointed and glistens with God's favor. Jesus' mission was to preach the reign of God. Christ himself, anointed with the oil of gladness, proclaims the love of God.

Water, oil, and fire are among the traditional symbols of the Holy Spirit. Of these three sacramentals, however, in the stories we have examined, fire correlates most directly with God the Holy Spirit. From the cosmic story we learned that fire captured from the Sun burns in cells and animates all living beings. As light, fire is the force that holds atoms and molecules together and causes everything to emanate light. As flame, God sent Moses from the desert to Egypt. Pentecost flames drove the disciples out of hiding to preach. The Spirit is the passion of

God that shines and burns as a fire within. The Spirit, as fire, transforms everything it touches. The Spirit is the force that drives us forward, finishes our prayers, and dwells as flames within our hearts. In baptism a person is born of water, anointed with oil, and indwelled by fire. Water, oil, fire—Creator, Christ, Spirit.

Cosmocentric Baptism

Now that we have highlighted some of the key points from the stories of water, oil, and fire, and have considered one facet of what the sacramentals reveal about God, we are ready to address baptism itself. We first consider baptism's cosmic history in light of Teilhard de Chardin's four developmental thresholds. We conclude this section on baptism with a reflection on the significance of a cosmocentric perspective for a community celebrating baptism.

Thresholds

In *The Human Phenomenon*, Pierre Teilhard de Chardin discusses the development of Earth in terms of crossing the four thresholds of pre-life, life, thought, and superlife.[1] As the previous chapters applied these thresholds to the sacramentals water, oil, and fire, we now apply them to baptism itself. While a review of the histories of the sacramentals is largely factual, the history of the sacrament is more allegorical. The construction of the prelife and life phases of baptism, therefore, draws on the baptismal tradition itself.

The pre-life phase of baptism may best be represented by Melito of Sardis, who (writing ca. 165) enthusiastically proclaims that all creation participates in a cosmic baptism. Recall this passage we quoted in the chapter on water:

> If you wish to observe the heavenly bodies being baptized, make haste now to the Ocean, and there I will show you a strange sight. If you look there you will see the heavenly bodies being baptized. At the end of the day they make haste to the Ocean, there to go down into the waters, into the outspread sea, and boundless main, and infinite deep, and immeasurable Ocean, and pure water. The sun sinks into the sea, and when it has been bathed in symbolic baptism, it comes up exultantly from the waters, rising

1. Pierre Teilhard de Chardin, *The Human Phenomenon*, trans. Sarah Appleton-Weber (Portland, OR: Sussex Academic Press, 2003).

as a new sun, purified from the bath. What the sun does, so do the stars and moon. They bathe in the sun's swimming pool like good disciples. By this baptism, sun, moon, and stars are soaking up pure brilliance.[2]

Moving into the life phase, Melito also speaks of the Earth bathed in rain, the air washed by raindrops, and the land renewed by the seasonal floods of the Nile River.[3]

The *Catechism of the Catholic Church*, in a section entitled "Prefigurations of Baptism in the Old Covenant," implies the prelife and life phases of baptism in the waters of creation and of the great flood. Suggesting a prelife phase, the *Catechism* says, "Since the beginning of the world, water . . . has been the source of life and fruitfulness." Quoting from the blessing of water, the *Catechism* continues, "At the very dawn of creation your Spirit breathed on the waters, making them the wellspring of all holiness" (1218). Suggesting the life phase of baptism, the *Catechism* says: "The Church has seen in Noah's ark a prefiguring of salvation by Baptism, for by it 'a few, that is eight persons, were saved through water'" (1219). The *Catechism* continues with the blessing of water, which says: "The waters of the great flood you made a sign of the waters of Baptism, that make an end of sin and a new beginning of goodness" (1219). Although the *Catechism* mentions only the human survivors of the flood, recall that pairs of every animal were also in the ark and that God's covenant, signified by the rainbow, was with all creatures. We read in Genesis: "When I bring clouds over the Earth and the bow is seen in the clouds, I will remember my covenant that is between me and you and every living creature of all flesh; and the waters shall never again become a flood to destroy all flesh" (Gen 9:14-15). In the "prefigurations" offered by the *Catechism* the primordial waters that preceded creation suggest the prelife phase of baptism. The waters of the flood, in their relationship with nonhuman as well as human creation, suggest the life phase of baptism.

The thought phase of baptism includes all the Scripture and tradition that leads to the current celebration of baptism. This phase is formed by its two-thousand-year Christian history and its seven-thousand-year Hebrew history. It also draws from thousands of years of human insight, millions of years of mammalian instinct, billions of years of life experience,

2. Quoted in Kilian McDonnell, *The Baptism of Jesus in the Jordan: The Trinitarian and Cosmic Order of Salvation* (Collegeville, MN: Liturgical Press, 1996), 50–51.

3. Ibid., 51.

and many more billions of years of cosmic dynamics. This entire inheritance informed the choices early Christians made as they developed the sacrament of baptism and influenced how the contemporary church celebrates baptism today. Baptism will move into its superlife phase as sacramental ministers and theologians become profoundly aware of the depth of their tradition.

Baptism begins to cross the threshold into superlife, its cosmocentric phase, as the church community becomes aware of the continuity of God's blessing throughout the Universe and the continuity of the story of the Universe with baptism. The cosmocentric phase of baptism recognizes that all the beings in the Universe already and perpetually receive and respond to God's blessing. Baptism does not mark the first moment when God becomes present to a person. God is intimately part of every person from the beginning of her life and through the entire 13.7 billion years that made that life possible. Baptism, rather, is a celebration of God's relationship with the Universe and the individual person in both the moment of her baptism and throughout the entire cosmic history. Baptism is also a thanksgiving for the future in which divine presence can never be lost. Each person is continuous with the Universe in its history, in its present moment, and in its future possibilities. Baptism celebrates the relationship God has with each being from the Beginning to the end of time.

In the cosmocentric phase of baptism, three blessings are celebrated: the blessing creation received at the Beginning, the blessing creation received at Jesus' baptism, and the blessing an individual receives at her baptism. Baptism celebrates her 13.7-billion-year process of creation and God calls her good. It celebrates the kinship she shares with God and the Earth community. Baptism is the celebration of the presence of the God aflame in her heart.

A sacrament requires not only a blessing, but also a response. The newly-baptized person's response is to acknowledge the lighted candle she receives and to tend it. The flame she tends does not reside solely in her heart, but burns in each and every member of the community around her. To be attentive to the presence of the Spirit within her she must grow in her ability to be responsive to the presence of the Spirit all around her. She tends the flame of her baptism as she grows in compassion and awareness of the sacredness of the Earth community in all its struggles and joys. Everything is joined in the thriving and struggling of the Universe and the Earth community. Water teaches her that all beings are created and sustained by the same source. Oil teaches her that her sensitivity is for the sake of the entire Earth community. Fire teaches her to notice the presence of the Spirit glowing in all things. The sacramentals teach that nothing is alone. Her cosmocentric baptism proclaims her sacred depths that originate in the blessing of the world at its creation and flow to her through the baptism of Jesus. Her response is to celebrate that same sacredness in the Earth community.

Celebration

The rubrics for a cosmocentric celebration of baptism would be much the same as those currently described in *The Rites of the Catholic Church*. The difference between the cosmocentric and current celebrations arises from a deepened awareness of and connection to the cosmic and sacred expressions of water, oil, and fire. The prayer over the baptismal water would recall the blessing water received at the beginning and tell of its role in salvation history from the birth of the Universe to the present moment. It reminds the people gathered that all water, the water in the font, the water in local streams, the water in the beings around them, as well as the water in their own bodies, flows with blessing.

As the person being baptized senses the water on her head she feels the cleansing rains, streams, and floods of all time wash over her. She is cleansed of the separation caused by believing and behaving as though she were anything other than a vibrant member of the Body of Christ, deeply embedded in the Earth community.

As the priest puts his thumb into the holy oil he knows that he is dipping into nothing less than the generosity of olives, the self-sacrifice of all plants, and the sensitivity of every living being. He is keenly aware that this oil carries the gift and responsibility of compassion on behalf of the Earth community. As he anoints this newly-baptized person he sees her shining face and knows that the oil he puts on her forehead magnifies what is already there.

As her godparents hand her a lighted candle they see its light and the light that emanates from everything in the church. They sense the candle's breath and the flames breathing in their own cells. In the candle they feel the store of Earth's energy that will be released by the light of their godchild—a candle given, a life given in return. They know that the candle, even untended, will continue to burn. More importantly, they know that if the flame is tended, followed, and fed, the adventure that awaits their godchild and the gift she will bring to the Earth and the Universe are unfathomable.

SACRAMENTALITY

Having reflected on the sacramentals of baptism and the significance of the integration of their stories to a cosmocentric celebration of baptism, we now turn to sacramentality in general. This section is presented in two parts: "Reflections on Sacramentals" and "Cosmocentric Sacramentality." In the first part we apply what we have learned from water, oil, and fire to the sacramentals in the other six ritual sacraments. We then reflect on the sacramental nature of other objects inside and outside the church. In the second part we apply the four Teilhardian thresholds to sacramentality and then conclude with a reflection on the essence of sacramental response, suggesting that the particular response asked of humanity seems to be the deepening of compassion.

Reflections on Sacramentals

To achieve a full appreciation of the significance of the integration of the stories of the sacramentals to a cosmocentric sacramentality, we would need to investigate all the sacramentals. Bread and wine, gold rings and white garments all have stories that provide unique insights into the celebrations in which they participate, and into the divine. The less-noticed sacramentals—such as ritual words and liturgical books, chalices and patens, altars and ambos, vessels and corporals—also warrant consideration. Many of these have unique histories that include everything from who currently cares for them and who crafted them to the history of that craft and where the materials originated. To include all the sacramentals in the church, such things as presiders' chairs and pews, as well as tabernacles and processional crosses, stained glass windows and wall coverings, marble steps, and even lowly carpeting would require exploration. All of these things used in worship are sacramentals whose stories, if heard, reveal aspects of the divine mystery. Not everything we learn from sacramentals is glorious, however. The mining of gold for a particular chalice may have caused mercury leaching. The wood for a set of pews may have been harvested by clear-cutting an old-growth forest. The carpeting under an altar may have been made of petroleum-based synthetics in an abusive sweatshop. Like the people who fill the pews, the sacramentals that fill the church carry joys as well as sorrows. Stories of life, death, and resurrection resonate through every corner. Even before the sacristan arrives to turn on the lights for morning Mass the church is full of stories of divine mystery yearning to be read. Learning to read these stories and apply what we discover to our sacramental celebrations is the beginning of a cosmocentric sacramentality.

Sacramentals are not confined within the walls of the church. Objects that enhance our worship are also encountered throughout the local community of life. Recall that when Jesus stepped into the waters of the Jordan all water rippled with the joy of this blessing. The holy water near church doors and in cruets waiting to be added to the eucharistic cup surely knows this blessing, as does the water in the puddles in the church parking lot, the water that gives life to the squirrels on the church lawn, and the water served at dinner. The blessing of water, of creation, flows into every aspect of our lives and the lives of every being we encounter. Water, oil, and fire, as well as bread and wine and even carpet reveal the mystery of God no matter where or when we meet them. Everything we encounter is endowed with the capacity to reveal God and mediate grace. Becoming aware of the cosmic and sacred stories of the beings with whom we share our lives and our worship enhances our ability to recognize and respond to God's constant blessing. Our knowledge of God supervenes upon our knowledge of the created world. As Thomas Aquinas wrote: "the opinion is false of those who asserted that it makes no difference to the truth of faith what anyone holds about creatures, so long as one thinks rightly about God . . . for error concerning creatures spills over into false opinion about God."[4] Building on Thomas's insight, we affirm that the more intimately we know the beings that surround us, the more clearly we can see the God they reveal.

Cosmocentric Sacramentality

The members of the Earth community participate in sacramentality not only by revealing God and mediating God's blessing but also by responding to God's constant blessing. A cosmocentric view of sacramentality includes the idea that neither blessing nor response to blessing began with humans but were already present in the cosmos at the Beginning. We see in the Genesis account of creation that God's blessing begins on the first day of creation; it does not wait for the creation of humans. Earth's response to God's blessing is evident in the beauty of the Earth drawn out of molten magma in the emergence of life. As Brian Swimme says, "the Earth was once molten rock and now sings opera."[5] To understand

---

4. Thomas Aquinas, *Summa Contra Gentiles* II, q. 3, a. 6.
5. Quoted in Neal Rogin and Drew Dellinger, "Earth and Life," *The Awakening Universe*, DVD, directed by Neal Rogin (San Francisco: The Pachamama Alliance, 2006).

this profound emergent process in Earth's evolution, this section begins with a look at sacramentality in terms of the Teilhardian thresholds of development. We then conclude this book with thoughts on the role of nature and the unique contribution asked of the human community by a cosmocentric sacramentality.

Thresholds

One last time we return to Teilhard de Chardin's four thresholds as a framework for understanding Earth's development, this time applying them to sacramentality itself. The passage of sacramentality through each threshold of development from pre-life to life, to thought, to super-life, corresponds to an ever-increasing ability to respond to the eternally present blessing of God.

In the pre-life stage, which extends some thirteen billion years from the Beginning through the formation of life in Earth's oceans, the response to God's blessing was manifested primarily on an atomic and molecular level. Through the fundamental interactions of gravity, the nuclear-strong interaction, and electromagnetism, particles of matter first formed nuclei and atoms and then galaxies, stars, and planets. The urge to respond to the ordering principles of the Universe is primordial. This tendency in all matter is the most ancient form of response to God's blessing of creation and so, at least in an allegorical sense, is the most primeval expression of sacramentality. This ancient resonance with divine blessing—Irenaeus's first anointing—did not end when Earth crossed the threshold into life. Rather, the responsiveness of matter to the fundamental interactions continues to bind and sustain creation.

The life stage of sacramentality began when the first being came to life in Earth's ancient womb. God's desire to create drew the response of diversification from early life. Fossil evidence suggests that the first fervor of life may have resulted in the most diverse population of living beings the planet has ever known.[6] Since its birth, life on Earth has formed and reformed in response to the blessing of new sources of energy and new habitats as well as in response to extinctions and the subsequent possibility for new beginnings. As the animals in our human lineage coevolved with their environments, new modes of sensitivity emerged. From primitive single-celled beings with sensitive membranes we inherited the senses of

6. Stephen Jay Gould, *Wonderful Life: The Burgess Shale and the Nature of History* (New York: W. W. Norton, 1989).

touch and smell. We inherited our sight from ancient fish whose sensitivity to sunlight originated in their photosynthetic ancestors. The sensitivity to sounds offered to mammalian ears first evolved in lizards who used their jawbones to perceive vibrations moving through the ground. These and so many other developments in sensitivity enabled the creatures of the Earth community to respond more deeply to the creative blessing of God expressed in the complexification of the planet. In the life phase, primordial sacramentality becomes sentient.

Crossing the threshold into the thought phase of Earth's development, sacramentality became self-aware. Before there were sacred rituals, ancient humans may have looked at the Moon and stood in awe. They may have tasted a fruit and smiled in gratitude. They may have danced with joy when a child was born and again when that child became an adult. The earliest direct evidence of ritual, and perhaps sacramentality, comes from a Neanderthal burial site more than fifty thousand years old, where the deceased was buried with food and stones painted in red ochre.[7] Many thousands of years later, sacred rituals from Mediterranean cultures contributed first to the development of Jewish and then Christian expressions of response to divine blessing.

All of human history since the dawn of writing has taken place within the thought phase of Teilhard's thresholds, a history that includes the developments in sacramentality that culminate thus far in the careful delineation of the ritual sacraments. This phase includes the condensation of sacramental expression that was well on its way to uniformity by the eighth century, as evidenced in the Gelasian Sacramentary and the freezing of sacramental practice in the sixteenth century by the Council of Trent in response to the challenge of the Reformation. The thought phase also saw twentieth-century sacramentality flow beyond its ritual expression to include an understanding of Jesus and the church as sacraments, and even the cosmos as sacramental. Sacramentality approaches the threshold into superlife when thoughts of a sacramental world yield to experiences of intimacy that restore the continuity between humanity and the rest of creation.

The superlife or cosmocentric phase of sacramentality requires the deepening of sensitivities acquired in the previous phases. In the pre-life phase, molecular sensitivity emerged; in the life phase came ecological

7. Brian Swimme and Thomas Berry, *The Universe Story: From the Primordial Flaring Forth to the Ecozoic Era—a Celebration of the Unfolding of the Cosmos* (San Francisco: HarperSanFrancisco, 1992), 152.

sensitivity; in the thought phase, cognitive sensitivity emerged. Cosmo-centric sacramentality requires the emergence of sensitivity capable of experiencing sacramentality from a cosmic rather than a merely human perspective. This phase is distinguished from the thought phase in that it cannot be entered solely through cognitive effort. Cognition can approach this threshold but cannot cross it. The knowing required here is experiential and must be grown into rather than simply figured out. That is, we have entered the cosmocentric phase of sacramentality to the extent that we actually experience ourselves as part of a sacred cosmos. As the discontinuity between humanity and the rest of creation heals, our ability to learn from creation and then to integrate this learning into our experience of God and sacramentality deepens.

The ability to learn from creation extends not only to the sacramentals and to sacramentality in general, but also to each of the seven ritual sacraments. Reflection on insights drawn from the cosmos and the Earth community would be part of a cosmocentric preparation for the celebration of every sacrament. For instance, in cosmocentric preparation for a baptismal celebration we invite reflection on the way novelty runs through each of the Teilhardian phases. Preparation for Eucharist requires an intimate inquiry into how Earth feeds and nourishes itself and suggests contemplation of the role of sacrifice in the Universe. Reconciliation calls for reflection on how Earth heals. Confirmation invites investigation into the ways young members of the Earth community become adults and how they benefit from the learning of previous generations. Preparation for marriage involves a search for patterns of bonding throughout the Universe, whereas preparation for holy orders is deepened by examining how the dedication of a particular member of a community contributes to the good of the whole. Finally, anointing of the sick invites reflection on how life, death, and new life appear in the cosmos.

When we understand our own stories within the context of the cosmic story as well as understanding the fourteen-billion-year history of the sacramentals we open ourselves to a powerfully new sense of integral sacramentality. Not only does this enhance our experience of an individual sacramental celebration, it also deepens sacramental awareness in each of our lives.

Our own desire for God is a continuation of an inclination that has been part of the Universe since the beginning. As John Haught writes: "Modern science has also demonstrated that our roots still extend deep down into the Earth and fifteen billion years back in time to the big bang. Hence, our own hoping carries with it the whole universe's yearning for its future."[8] He continues: "Billions of years before our appearance in evolution it was already seeded with promise. Our own religious longing for future fulfillment, therefore, is not a violation but a blossoming of this promise."[9] Religious sacramentality is not simply a human construction, but a human expression of what the Universe has been about all along. Saint Paul writes that creation too is yearning toward completion in God. Haught tells us: "God is the creative *eros* that rouses the world to evolutionary movement."[10] All of creation, stars, planets, and humans, embody this urge toward greater beauty and fulfillment in God. We are the manifestation of this *eros* in human form. As we have seen, our own bodies pulse with the energy and matter created at the Beginning.

Integrating the cosmic and sacred stories of sacramentals and sacraments has the reciprocal effect of bringing an awareness of the Earth community to the celebration of the sacraments as well as bringing a sacramental appreciation to the celebration of life. Everything we encounter in our daily lives is worthy of our contemplation of the unique way it reveals the divine. Simply appreciating the blessing of water and being grateful for it wherever it appears is a practice worth cultivating. In the fascination of different beings—whether water, stars, or red-tailed hawks—the habit of noticing the particular beings who teach us draws us more deeply into resonance with a cosmos that radiates divine blessing. The practice of learning from Earth allows us to experience ourselves as students and peers of other members of the Earth community. It teaches us the humility to relinquish our role as masters, or even as stewards, of creation. Creation itself is the revelation of God. As we read the book of creation and as we feel ourselves part of it, not set above but embedded within it, the phase of cosmocentric sacramentality unfolds within us. Only time will tell us just how the cosmocentric phase of sacramentality will unfold. We are just now glimpsing across the threshold. Based on what we already know of the development of Earth, we can expect our sensitivity to the cosmos to increase along with our receptivity to the blessing it mediates.

Comprehensive Compassion

Once we see ourselves as embedded in creation, one species among the more than ten million alive today, and once we relinquish our sovereignty,

8. John Haught, *The Promise of Nature: Ecology and Cosmic Purpose* (New York: Paulist Press, 1993), 109.

9. Ibid.

10. Ibid., 33.

we can begin to appreciate the unique contributions humanity is able to make. When we experience the cosmos as revelatory and embrace it as sacred, as the body of Christ, have we any choice but to treat each member of the Earth community as kin and to make certain that all of our relationships are life-giving?

Cosmic evolution is producing a deepening capacity for compassion.[11] From atoms to life to self-reflective consciousness, Earth's ability to feel is expanding. Other creatures may have the capacity to care deeply, but humans are the only ones that can know the stories of all other species and so are the only species who can care for the children of all species. It is unlikely that even the most well-intentioned dolphins can know anything about the plight of mountain gorillas. Humans, however, because of our ability to communicate around the globe, can sense and care about beings wherever we find them. Without overstretching the point, we may speculate that there are likely to be extremophiles that live in geysers and beneath the ocean floor and such places that humans will never know about. Only God can care at that depth. Nevertheless, humans have the capacity to extend the compassion of Earth further than any other species. Only humans can love the entire planet and try to prevent harm from coming to the beloved. Human choices will, to a large extent, determine the fate of the biosphere. Which species will survive and which ones will perish is now in our hands. A cosmocentric sacramental appreciation of Earth compels us to make choices for the benefit of the Earth community, not because it is in our best interest or only because it is the right thing to do, but because we have fallen in love.

11. Comprehensive compassion is a concept developed by Brian Swimme that gives evidence for the deepening capacity of care in the Universe. For more on this topic see Susan Bridle, "Comprehensive Compassion: An Interview with Brian Swimme," in *What is Enlightenment?* 19, *Can Enlightenment Save the World?* (Spring-Summer 2001), 34–42, 133–35.

BIBLIOGRAPHY

Ball, Philip. *Life's Matrix: A Biography of Water*. Berkeley: University of California Press, 2001.

Berry, Thomas. *The Dream of the Earth*. San Francisco: Sierra Club Books, 1988.

Boskou, Dimitrios, ed. *Olive Oil: Chemistry and Technology*. Champaign, IL: AOCS Press, 1996.

Braud, William, and Rosemarie Anderson. *Transpersonal Research Methods for the Social Sciences: Honoring Human Experience*. Thousand Oaks, CA: Sage Publications, 1998.

Bridle, Susan. "Comprehensive Compassion: An Interview with Brian Swimme." *What is Enlightenment?* 19, *Can Enlightenment Save the World?* (Spring-Summer 2001), 34–42, 133–35.

Bryson, Bill. *A Short History of Nearly Everything*. New York: Random House, 2003.

Chaisson, Eric. *Epic of Evolution: Seven Ages of the Cosmos*. New York: Columbia University Press, 2006.

Delsemme, Armand. *Our Cosmic Origins: From the Big Bang to the Emergence of Life and Intelligence*. Cambridge: Cambridge University Press, 1998.

Early Lighting: A Pictorial Guide. Hartford, CT: The Rushlight Club, 1972.

Eiseley, Loren. *The Star Thrower*. New York: Harcourt Brace, 1978.

Fagg, Lawrence W. *Electromagnetism and the Sacred: At the Frontier of Spirit and Matter*. New York: Continuum, 1999.

Faraday, Michael. *The Chemical History of a Candle*. New York: Dover Publications, 2002.

Freedman, Roger A., and William J. Kaufmann. *Universe*. 6th ed. New York: W. H. Freeman, 2002.

Gould, Stephen Jay. *Wonderful Life: The Burgess Shale and the Nature of History*. New York: W. W. Norton, 1989.

Haught, John. *The Promise of Nature: Ecology and Cosmic Purpose*. New York: Paulist Press, 1993.

Keller, Catherine. *Face of the Deep: A Theology of Becoming*. New York: Routledge, 2005.

Kilmartin, Edward J. "Theology of the Sacraments: Toward a New Understanding of the Chief Rites of the Church of Jesus Christ." In *Alternative Futures for Worship*. Edited by Regis A. Duffy, 123–75. Collegeville, MN: Liturgical Press, 1987.

Kiritsakis, Apostolos. *Olive Oil: From the Tree to the Table*. 2d ed. Trumbull, CT: Food & Nutrition Press, 1998.

Kittel, Gerhard, Geoffrey W. Bromiley, and Gerhard Friedrich, eds. *Theological Dictionary of the New Testament*. 10 volumes. Grand Rapids: Eerdmans, 1964.

MacGregor, A. J. *Fire and Light in the Western Triduum: Their Use at Tenebrae and at the Paschal Vigil*. Collegeville, MN: Liturgical Press, 1992.

Marrin, West. *Universal Water: The Ancient Wisdom and Scientific Theory of Water*. Makawao, Maui, HI: Inner Ocean Publishing, 2002.

Martin, George C. "Botany of the Olive." In *Olive Production Manual*. Edited by G. Steven Sibbett, Louise Ferguson, and George Martin. Oakland, CA: University of California, Division of Agriculture and Natural Resources, Publication 3353, 1994.

McDonnell, Kilian. *The Baptism of Jesus in the Jordan: The Trinitarian and Cosmic Order of Salvation*. Collegeville, MN: Liturgical Press, 1996.

Milani, Jean P., Biological Sciences Curriculum Study, et al. *Biological Science: A Molecular Approach*. 6th ed. Lexington, MA: D. C. Heath, 1990.

Morris, Emma, and Jane Zipp, eds. *Thomas Berry: The Great Story*. DVD, directed by Nancy Stetson and Penny Morrell. Oley, PA: Bullfrog Films, 2002.

Mukherjee, N. R. "Flames." *Encyclopaedic Dictionary of Physics: General, Nuclear, Solid State, Molecular Chemical, Metal and Vacuum Physics, Astronomy, Geophysics, Biophysics, and Related Subjects*. Edited by J. Thewlis, et al., 164–68. New York: Pergamon Press, 1961.

Osborne, Kenan B. *Christian Sacraments in a Postmodern World: A Theology for the Third Millennium*. New York: Paulist Press, 1999.

Palmer, Paul F., ed. *Sacraments and Worship: Liturgy and Doctrinal Development of Baptism, Confirmation, and the Eucharist*. Sources of Christian Theology 1. Westminster, MD: Newman Press, 1955.

Plotkin, Bill. *Soulcraft: Crossing into the Mysteries of Nature and Psyche*. Novato, CA: New World Library, 2003.

Rahner, Karl. *Foundations of Christian Faith: An Introduction to the Idea of Christianity*. New York: Seabury Press, 1978.

Relethford, John. *The Human Species: An Introduction to Biological Anthropology*. 5th ed. New York: McGraw Hill, 2003.

Robins, F. W. *The Story of the Lamp (and the Candle)*. New York: Oxford University Press, 1939.

Rogin, Neal, and Drew Dellinger. *The Awakening Universe*. DVD. San Francisco: The Pachamama Alliance, 2006.

Rosenblum, Mort. *Olives: The Life and Lore of a Noble Fruit*. New York: North Point Press, 1996.

Rost, Thomas L., Michael G. Barbour, C. Ralph Stocking, and Terence M. Murphy. *Plant Biology*. Davis, CA: Wadsworth, 1998.

Schaff, Philip, and Henry Wace, eds. *Nicene and Post-Nicene Fathers*. 2nd ed. Volume 7. New York: Hendrickson Publishers, 1999.

Schillebeeckx, Edward. *Christ the Sacrament of the Encounter with God*. New York: Sheed and Ward, 1963.

Silk, Joseph. *The Big Bang*. 3d ed. New York: W. H. Freeman and Company, 2001.

Swimme, Brian, and Thomas Berry. *The Universe Story: From the Primordial Flaring Forth to the Ecozoic Era—A Celebration of the Unfolding of the Cosmos*. San Francisco: HarperSanFrancisco, 1992.

Teilhard de Chardin, Pierre. *Toward the Future*. New York: Harcourt Brace Jovanovich, 1975.

———. "Mass on the World." In idem, *The Heart of Matter*, 119–34. New York: Harcourt Brace Jovanovich, 1978.

———. *The Human Phenomenon*. Translated by Sarah Appleton-Weber. Portland, OR: Sussex Academic Press, 2003.

Thomas Aquinas. *On the Truth of the Catholic Faith: Summa Contra Gentiles*. Book 2: *Creation*. Translated by James F. Anderson. Garden City, NY: Hanover House, 1956.

Thurman, Harold V., and Alan P. Trujillo. *Essentials of Oceanography*. 7th ed. Upper Saddle River, NJ: Prentice Hall, 2002.

Thurston, Herbert. "Paschal Candle." *The Catholic Encyclopedia*. Edited by Charles Herbermann, Conde Pallen, Thomas Shahan, and John Wynne. New York: Appleton, 1911.

Ward, Peter D., and Donald Brownlee. *Rare Earth: Why Complex Life is Uncommon in the Universe*. New York: Copernicus, 2000.

Wilson, H. A., ed. *The Gelasian Sacramentary: Liber Sacramentorum Romanae Ecclesiae*. Oxford: Clarendon Press, 1894.

Zajonc, Arthur. *Catching the Light: The Entwined History of Light and Mind*. Oxford: Oxford University Press, 1993.

SUBJECT INDEX

SCRIPTURAL INDEX